A New Mission

A New Mission

A New Mission

By *Terry Leaman*

- *A Mission into Life*

- *A Mission into Countries*

- *A Mission by God to Reach His People*

A New Mission

Copyright © 2017 By T.M.Leaman
A New Mission
All rights reserved

Index

Foreword by the Author	Page 7	
Preface	Page 11	

Chapter

1. A New Mission's Beginning — Page 17
2. A New 'Me' Beginning — Page 27
3. The Backwater — Page 42
4. Out of the Blue — Page 56
5. Follow the Pillar of Fire — Page 66
6. Do it Again Lord — Page 76
7. A Widening Mission — Page 86
8. A Hiccup in the Mission? — Page 92
9. Providing Help — Page 101
10. A Mission's Full Purpose — Page 113
11. What do you Preach? — Page 122
12. Radio Ministry and other things — Page 138
13. Products of Preaching — Page 146
14. The Risen Lord — Page 153

Photo Album — Page 164

15. The Mission if the Heart of God — Page 176
16. Jerusalem, Judea, Samaria & the uttermost parts of the earth — Page 187

A New Mission

Mission means 'to send' and comes from the Latin text. It was first used about 'missionaries' in the 16th century who went abroad building schools and missions.

A New Mission

Foreword by the Author

If I don't get this written down now or soon, I may forget some of the detail, either now or in the future, which just should not happen because what has happened in my life, to me anyway, is amazing. As an ordinary person, in my eyes at least, not out of the ordinary, without many special abilities, to see what has been done, is quite extraordinary. We often don't understand what we can be or what we can do. When God is part of the equation however, things can be so different. I wonder do we ever, even as born again people, realise what transpired within us when we made that simple but profound step of requesting God that He change us and clean us from our old ways and cleanse our old lives and make something new of them, doing what we think He may be capable of, to remake us in some way?

I never realised, in my wildest or widest thoughts, that I could achieve what God enabled me to achieve. We seem to think that life is only about us, not what could happen if the 'God factor' were involved. It's also interesting that things in early life, even very early life, even pre-birth life,

A New Mission

changed my destiny and made ready my thinking for what would follow many years on. If God readies us for His purposes, which for the raw me had to be so, then we need to look deeper at who we are and what we are because in His hands, the transition from fairly useless to really useful is simply a marvel. What are weaknesses can often suddenly transform into real assets in His hands. Attitudes that can be uninteresting to people of our race can often become very necessary to have to people of other races, even desirable.

I never cease to wonder how some of my less interesting ways seem even vital to what God required when He took me to do things in Africa and other places. It seems that even my personal features are an asset when out on God's work, whereas at home, people pass by without a glance. In fact the feeling that the only factor that makes a difference between mediocrity and usefulness is the God given part. It is He that changes things and makes things useful. We are just clay in His hands, and yet, the odd thing is, He whispers things in our ears that give us the courage, inclination and direction that somehow make us understand that, you know, maybe something can

A New Mission

be done with this personality, this character, that could actually become an asset?

It's hard to describe the feeling, the method He uses, the motivation, the teasing towards the goal, the drawing in of our wills toward His purpose that never pushes us too hard but even uses our own wishes to bring about what is nothing less than a vital part of His master plan. I'm reminded of God's question to the prophet in Ezekiel 37, "Son of man, can these bones live?" God teases out of Ezekiel the information that's inside Him. God has that questioning technique that He seems to use when He wants us to become something that we aren't yet or could know how to be, that as yet we don't understand. It's just amazing to me that God could know something about us that we are totally unaware of and then gradually draw those abilities out that only He recognises and knows how to foster.

If this book is about anything, it's not about what *we* can do but that God can do anything through us when we lend ourselves to His purposes. God took me by surprise so many times and in so many ways to produce a spiritual output. When it happened,

A New Mission

was it difficult? Was it frightening? Was it embarrassing? No it was an adventure. Would I do it again? **Yes please**.

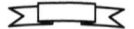

A New Mission

Preface

What IS it that God wants people to know, whether here at home (wherever home is for you) or in other countries? And HOW can He affect their lives such that they come to understand who they really ARE instead of what they are NOT, that the world, their flesh and Satanic forces have taught them that they are, that makes them fail in all that they do?

I always knew that there was a great way to live, that God had all the answers for us and that they were just a small distance away and could be grasped somehow ..... If only ....? The 'why's and wherefore's' seemed elusive for a while until I realised *I* had to take a part but there's the rub. If you're timid, shy and fearful, there doesn't seem ever to be a time in your life when you can see yourself doing those 'right things' that your soul would revel in and enjoy doing things that you know would satisfy God.

So where do you start? Fear stops you at the first object that appears in your path. Your own flesh cries out in negativity and presents all sorts of

A New Mission

excuses why you shouldn't even try to do stuff that's, well, 'beyond your reach as a person' and that 'you'll never complete the project, because you never finish anything do you?' Then the world around you presents another obstacle because they all know you to be too weak to present a credible challenge to the world's problems, even if you are a born again believer because they don't understand that bit either. But what's nice is that God has an interest in you. Really? Yes, He can do ***anything*** with ***anyone***. He really can! What? Even with someone like me? YES, especially you because those of us that don't have much confidence in ourselves apparently are sometimes easier to convince that God can help them and are often more malleable and open to being helped.

But whatever backgrounds we have, they're not always conducive to being Missionaries to anywhere, to help people of differing needs and races, so yes, there may be further hurdles to get over. Fears about dangerous insects, diseases, predators, animal or humans can be great deterrents especially if your inclinations and aspirations are low anyway. Some 'missions' into

A New Mission

the world seem impossible almost, until, that is, God steps into your world. Then the intrigue, the fascination, the allure of things that He highlights, enters your thinking. Then the other stuff seems to disappear in a haze ***and suddenly the impossible takes a back seat.........***

A New Mission

A New Mission

TO GOD WHO MAKES MY LIFE RIGHT

A New Mission

CHAPTER ONE

A NEW MISSION'S BEGINNING

Unbeknown to me, as I was still in the womb, possible forces against me were trying to eliminate my beginnings. My mother had become pregnant and being older than was advisable to have a child at that time and as I remember when I was young, always rather a slight lady, questions were asked about whether this pregnancy was a good idea. My parents were good, God fearing people, my father was a man of real faith and my mother a quiet, gentle woman with good morals and sensibilities. Neither of them, I can tell you, would normally consider aborting a child unless there were good reason but nevertheless there was real concern and did indeed make it a consideration.

At that time our church had a great Pastor, a man of dynamic faith who had raised the dead while on a mission in New Zealand. Pastor John Hewitt had been told by God to go on a mission and hold a crusade in an area that involved crossing a Maori

A New Mission

Chief's land. The Chief's daughter had been taken ill and died and all possibility of crossing his land was out of the question at that time. Pastor Hewitt asked to see his daughter and when shown in to the house, prayed for her and she was immediately raised up. This was the man of faith involved here.

When he was approached with my parents 'situation', he immediately said, "Lets go away for 3 days and pray, then we'll come together again". After the 3 day period, they returned together and the Pastor said clearly, "God has told me, 'Do nothing about this baby, this child is for the salvation of his family'!" And so the die was cast, this baby came into the world.

I didn't learn of these things until much later in life, when my father confided in my wife. I secretly believe he wanted me to know about it, as it would affect my future faith development and inform me about my life's purpose. It did just that. I never resented anything at all about it but instead knew that my life had a reason. Even in this God managed my affairs well, knowing just the right time of life to keep me informed of the things He wanted me to know.

A New Mission

Life seemed great as a youngster. I was privileged to have a good family, two older brothers to look up to and people were very kind to me. My favourite times of course were birthdays and Christmas like most children, when, unlike children born during the war, things were in much more abundance in my era.

I missed the war years thankfully and grew up in a time when all sorts of Technical developments were taking place. I had the privilege of seeing all the latest innovations coming out of the post war period. Electronics and sound and vision were the most fascinating to me of all the new advancements that were appearing and it would affect my career choices later on.

Being brought up with Christian parents I heard all the stories of the bible and naturally the subject of God and His goodness wasn't far away at any time. My mother would take me to bed at night and 'tuck me in' but before that, we would kneel by my bed and pray. My mother taught me to pray a simple prayer, quite common I believe to many children at that time. It followed the lines of a hymn.... "Gentle Jesus, meek and mild, look upon

A New Mission

this little child, pity my simplicity, suffer me to come to thee". Then would follow the words, "God bless Daddy, God bless Mummy, God bless Keith and Glyn (my 2 older brothers) and make me a good boy". It's funny but even at that early age (What? 4 years old?) I can remember saying those words and one evening really meaning that last line, "Make me a good boy!" As far as I can recall, I hadn't been a 'bad' boy that day but the words had a particular emphasis that evening and they sounded very sincere as I said them. There was something about God that was good above all else and I think in my mind or rather even deeper in my heart, I wanted some of that nature. It sounded wholesome and although I could never express it right or understand what I was saying at that juncture, I felt I was saying something, even something profound, that evening. I couldn't read or write much just then but my heart said something I couldn't even comprehend, being so young but something began right there. You know even now, in later life, our hearts can grasp things our heads can't get a handle on and hearing things, we say, "Mmmmm, there's just something about that…..".

A New Mission

Years went by, schooling began and I was a happy kid. Life was good. I progressed like the other kids and all seemed good. After a few years however, I found schooling wasn't quite so kind and soon the 'birds of the air' would peck once more at my right to exist and try and take the goodness out of what had been lovingly planted there.

At around 7 years of age my teachers decided that as I was coping so very well with school and as my birthday was in August, they thought I could easily transfer up to a higher class. I could remember in class always being the first with my hand up, eager to answer questions, understanding everything and doing well in all my subjects, enjoying the learning experience and growing up well and enthusiastically at that time.

Little did I know that my world would soon crumble around me and times of horror would come as I struggled to learn anything because I was now out of my depth in my new class, not knowing what the other children knew because I had skipped an entire year. I was now out on a limb and felt that the branch would break under

A New Mission

my weight. I now hid in the back of the class, in more ways than one, keeping my head down in case the teacher asked me a question that I couldn't answer, now losing all confidence and afraid of being found to be ignorant. In those days, if we were thought to be inattentive, we were often caned or severely reprimanded and I was afraid of the teachers thinking I hadn't been listening. I heard everything that was said, I just didn't understand it any more.

Corporal punishment was one of those things that made me fear, it was a painful experience and I remember many times the semi-subconscious feeling that the punishments were not because I deserved them but because I had been put in that position by others. I held my own however. Whether I was courageous deep down or just ignoring the circumstances, I just got on with what was before me and did my best.

I did have some high spots in life though. My reading abilities were good. In church we read the sometimes complex words found in the hymnal and the bible and often understood more than the other kids and I was well practiced and a good

A New Mission

reader, so once more God came to my rescue. On occasions, the teacher would ask the class one by one, to read excerpts from something and when my turn came, I would excel and my confidence would return somewhat until mathematics and other subjects would raise their heads again. I sat tight in many situations, keeping quiet and learned some patience in my trials. It took me a long time to catch up with my education, even until after I had left school, which I had to do, to put my career on track.

But there was another horror in my life. At the age of seven, also running alongside the education terror, I developed Asthma. I well remember going across the River Bridge in Newport where I was brought up. I enjoyed going to town and seeing the shops but one day as I ran and skipped along, an itching sensation began down inside my chest. It seemed to abate after a while but while we were on holiday some months later in Weymouth, as I was playing with a ball in the sea, thrashing about in the water and enjoying the sun, the horrible feeling returned. It brought with it an awful deprivation of breath leaving me gasping for air. I remember my mother walking me slowly to

A New Mission

Weymouth town to the pharmacist to get help and the chemist there saying, "There are only these", offering her a small white tablet which he said, "may not do very much good".

He was right, they did nothing for my days, and nights of hell began. There simply was no medication around then to help this condition and the inability to breathe at night began an era of sheer terror. What do you do when you can't get your breath and there's no remedy? How do you explain that to a little boy? Every night I lay so still as to not aggravate the condition and fear became the order of the day and night. It was like hiding from a predator that was after your life. You lay still in case it saw you. On the bad nights I sat up in bed and propped myself up in the most agreeable position where I could get the most breath. After many days of this all my arms, chest and sides would ache as I tried to draw in breath.

Alongside this I would hear things in church that would enter my conscious and subconscious world that would just give me a hope. I heard of those people in the bible and in modern times where they would testify that God had healed them if they

A New Mission

believed. I remember one night being unable to sleep or breathe well. I sat, propping myself up in bed to increase my air intake and as I did so, I started to say the name of Jesus in rhythm with my breathing, sort of calling on God for breath. It actually helped and I did it over and over with a little hope in me growing in the background all the while. That was the only way I felt I could live at night for many years.

God had again done something that no one else could do. I was beginning to trust Him and see that there were few in the world who were always dependable, when everything else failed. Of course all the bible stories in Sunday school bore out the same message that this God was someone you could trust with your life and I was bolstered in my faith by them.

A New Mission

CHAPTER TWO

A NEW 'ME' BEGINNING.

At the age of eleven I had come to a point that I felt deeply that I needed God, in more ways than medically. The things He had helped me with were convincing me more and more that He was the answer to my needs. I heard the gospel preached in church and longed to respond to the Pastors call to accept Jesus as my saviour and Lord but the fear in me prevented me from responding. The Pastor would say, "If you want Jesus to come into your life…, just raise your hand and show us that's what you want to do". I almost did it a few times but fear would back me off and I would slink out of church hoping no one would see me and confront me with the issue. The more I put it off, the less I wanted to face another altar call from the Pastor, the fear in me hated the idea of my asking God into my life. You know God knows more about us than we care to admit sometimes.

A New Mission

There was a young man that lived up the South Wales coast from Newport, someone I really looked up to. I used to see him at the church's annual international convention every year. I thought the young man was the coolest I had ever met. I don't know what it was about him but if I could have spent every hour listening to him and his mates talking, I would have but the week of the convention went too quickly and it was back to normal life and the same old drudge of sickness and school.

This one August though, the young man had work to do in my hometown selling custom made house signs and came to stay with us. I was made; this hope on my horizon had a serious possibility of raising my spirits and giving me a lift out of my humdrum life. Late that month he arrived and stayed for almost a week. He worked during the days and I went with him one afternoon and saw him at work but at night when we went to bed, we talked about boy's stuff. We talked about girls and football, cars and whatever the trend was then. I loved it.

A New Mission

Then one night as we lay in bed, the conversation was interrupted by a question I wasn't expecting. After a slight lull in the conversation, Philip said, "Terry, are you born again?" It caught me by surprise. I knew I wasn't born again, I hadn't responded to the gospel message and admitted my need for God publicly when it was preached and I knew that I needed to admit it to someone.

I may have had fear for all sorts of reasons but here God was putting salvation on a plate for me and letting me in where really I had no right to get in but that's God, gracious to the last, listening to my heart and not my fears. The question seemed to resound around the room and I put the young man off at first, again out of fear. "Yes I think so!" I said, hoping that would deter him, yet all the time my soul longed for it to be so. I *wanted* to be born again, I *knew* it was just what my life needed. "So why don't you make sure?" came his response. I immediately said, "Yes", before fear could change my mind, "I would like to!" Do you know that fear can change your mind? Just look at the disciples on the boat when the storm arose. In the height of the storm when their fear was at its greatest, they woke him as He slept in the back of

A New Mission

the boat and said to Him, "Don't you care that we perish?" Jesus was the most caring that they knew and was always protecting people from disease, sickness, demons etc, yet their language turned when fear arrived.)

So, when presented with an open option, I responded and stood against my fear. We got out from under the bedclothes and knelt by the side of my bed. We prayed the sinner's prayer together and I invited Jesus into my life. I remember the clean feeling that followed in the wake of the "Amen". I was saved, God had reached into my life and given me the one thing that my soul needed and deep down always wanted. There was that 'side of the bed' experience again. I had prayed there as a much younger lad with my mother a similar prayer in feeling but now I had made a conscious decision to say a full "Yes" to God and to His demands on my life...... And it felt GOOD!

The years went by and I often struggled in school physically. I loved sports, especially swimming and riding my bike but breath often eluded me and I had to keep to a lot of 'quiet' and sedentary

A New Mission

pastimes. A few times I nearly died. One day, loving to swim, I went on a sunny afternoon to an outdoor lido with a friend, a lay Pastor and his family. I dived into the water at the earliest opportunity, which was very cold and I barely made it to the bank. It took all my breath from me and I remember the desperate feeling of having no air. This lay Pastor from our church, Daniel, pulled me out of the water and lay by me and prayed for me. I remember him speaking to the asthmatic condition and rebuking it. I had never heard anyone do that before. The symptoms alleviated quickly as he spoke and I sat gasping at the air. That was a close one. On another occasion I got into difficulty while at his house after riding a bike and couldn't breathe. He took me into his garage. As a mechanic he had oxygen and acetylene cylinders for welding and turned on the oxygen in the torch and waved it across my mouth, saying, "breathe gently" as I inhaled the pure air. Again I recovered. God always seemed to come to my rescue; my faith in Him was growing.

I grew up and left school, passing some exams well and getting decent grades. My interest now

A New Mission

was in Sound Engineering, Radio and Television and Electronics. I soon got work as an engineer and 5 years later passed my 'finals' happily and qualified well. Life was beginning to take some shape.

The lean years were disappearing, there were even some asthma inhalers appearing in the National Health Service but they were not very effective for me. Doctors said that I would maybe grow out of the condition in my late teens but until the age of 27 when God healed me, I still suffered bad attacks.

After around 6 years of work and after qualifying as a Sound Engineer and Cable TV Engineer, I made a decision that I wanted to give more of my life to God. I just wanted to know more about Him. After all I had learned of Him in church through top preachers and in Sunday school as a child, it wasn't enough, there was just something about God that I needed to know more about. You know you can read about someone, hear the stories but never know them fully. I wanted to know more of the one that gave me hope and kept saving my life. So after a little thought I decided to sign

A New Mission

up for Bible College, it seemed to be a way of breaking out of my structured life and finding out more about this one, that I knew in my heart was the answer to many questions and the source of my faith.

As a sound engineer, I had taken on the responsibility for the Church's International Convention Hall sound system and translation facilities. I renovated it, designing, building and installing some of the electronic equipment myself, bringing it up to the newer standards. It was in the same area in West Wales in the UK where the Bible College was that I was about to attend in the September, so I got to know the area well.

As I joined the other students at the start of the academic term and spent the first nights in the dormitory, I encountered a real problem. The asthma attacks that I had been getting some small relief from, escalated and I spent night after night (sleeping on feather and flock pillows that are renowned for being bad for asthmatics) suffering every night, once more experiencing that awful feeling of being unable to breathe.

A New Mission

After 6 weeks I was severely weak. I remember one morning staggering like an old man to the lecture room some 500 metres away. It took about an hour to get there and when I reached the lecture room I flopped down in my seat at my desk, exhausted. The students were just finishing morning devotions when I arrived. Being fed up with this asthmatic condition that just dogged my life and angry that my faith seemed to be letting me down, I turned my attention to God and simply said aggressively to Him, ***"I've had enough. You HAVE to tell me something that will change this situation!"*** The slightly tongue in cheek way I said the words were almost on the edge of blasphemy for me, I had NEVER spoken to God like this before.

I had a surprise coming. God took no notice of my anger, which seemed to be pointed at Him but instead He seemed to reward the tenacity of my faith. As I said it, a thought came into my head **'get your Bible'**. I reached for the book on the bookshelf beside my desk and simply flipped it open. It fell open at 'Proverbs' Chapter 3 and I began reading at the first verse at the top of the left hand page. What it said hit me right between the

A New Mission

eyes. "It read, (verse 24) **"When you lie down, you shall not be afraid, you shall lie down and your sleep shall be sweet".** The words leapt out at me and I could not believe my eyes. Of all the verses in the Bible, (and as I understand it, no other verses said anything like this), yet I had opened to this one. How DID God do that? It wasn't as though I had read those pages before, or regularly, so the book opened there naturally. Once again, there was that hope, ploddingly following after me, and now a direct word from God, **exactly** fitting my situation.

I couldn't wait to get to bed that night. God had spoken right into my situation and I wanted to see what He would do. Even getting up onto my bunk and just putting my elbow on the feather and flock pillows created enough dust to start off another asthma attack as I breathed it in. Before anything else could happen I reached for the source of my new hope and read that scripture again. **"When you lie down…..",** there it was, just as dynamic and solid as when I read it earlier. As I read it and the Asthma ensued, anger rose inside me. I slammed the Bible shut and my Italian roommate jumped at the sound and said, "Whatsa going

A New Mission

onna?" I said in my righteous anger, "GOD SAID IT Santino, and I believe it, now I'm going to sleep!" there was an Italian "Amen" from him.

I furiously slammed my head down on the pillow making as much dust as I could, as if to say, 'You want dust? I'll give you dust'. I closed my eyes and in around 3 minutes, was fast asleep. ***You know when God speaks, He means what He says and what He says works!***

Every night for a week the same events happened. Every night I denied the Asthma any ground when it started and every night I slept soundly after slamming my head on the pillow. After a week I stopped reading the Bible because I knew what it said now and just went to sleep still making as much dust as I could, defying the awful sickness any rights. Sometimes even now, I still heavily hit the pillow, there's a sense of victory about it but I've never lost a night's sleep since due to Asthma. **God KEEPS His word.**

At the age of 27, I was prayed for again by my good friend and prophet Daniel and daytime

A New Mission

Asthma left too, that awful demon left me, another proof of God's love and care for us.

Those days set down a marker for my life and my faith, along with my father's life story, which was a remarkable tale of God's incredible goodness in which he witnessed many amazing miracles where people challenged sickness and disease with the words of God. These things all set me up for further adventure with Him.

It was while at the College that I had another 'God encounter'. Many may not have put much store on it but for me it was significant for a number of reasons. As a body of students, we decided on an outreach where we would put on a film in the local church hall and invite villagers to come and see it. The film, 'His Land' was a Billy Graham Ministries film and starred Cliff Richards in a Christian Musical about biblical prophecy. We discussed how best to go about getting local people along to see it and decided that the best method was to simply knock on doors and invite them. We split up into pairs and divided the local villages into sections, taking a section each.

A New Mission

A lad, a student from Scotland called Walker and myself had drawn a section of one of the villages nearby. We took all our leaflets and prayed before we went. We decided that we would go to every house and not leave any out. After covering most of our allotted houses, we had about 2 left to visit and approached the penultimate house. As we walked along towards the gate a large black dog emerged on the other side of the front wall, barking very aggressively. Walker immediately said, "I ain't going in there", in his broad Glaswegian accent. I replied tactfully, "Well we ***did*** say we would cover ***every*** house in our area." Walker grimaced and was not happy and even less enamoured when we approached the gate and put our hands on it, lifting the latch and seeing this dog develop into a crazed maniac of a beast. If it was 'upset' at our presence before, it was really not smitten with romance with our latest action. It escalated it's leaping and snarling, showing its teeth and becoming even more aggressive. Just then, as I said to Walker, "Come on, we ***did*** say we would go to EVERY house", I opened the gate and we entered the garden, closed the gate behind us. As I did so, a strange feeling of this being the **right** thing to do, came over me. Walker was still not

A New Mission

happy and I told him to stay close behind me, which he was extremely happy to do. We went up the path looking for the front door to the house as we did so. The door was on the side of the house and we both sighed heavily at the realisation of having to walk the extra distance with the attentions of this dog being SO aggressive.

The black dog charged at us time and time again, snarling at us and we could feel the hot breath on the back of our hands as it came within millimetres of biting us. ***But it didn't.*** It did ***everything but*** bite. We turned the corner of the house and there was the welcome sight of the door we had looked for. Once more, unbelievably, the dog upped its efforts to deter us and I grabbed the doorknocker and rapped it hard. As I did, a voice inside said, "Come in, it's open!" I opened the door and we pressed ourselves inside, shutting the door quickly behind us only to face a surprised householder sat at the kitchen table. "Oh. Sorry, I thought it was…..". His voice trailed off and he asked us why we were there. We explained our visit and gave him the invitation to see the film, which he thanked us for. We spoke for a short while and felt that we had done what we came to do.

A New Mission

We then turned to go out through the door again and face 'The Beast'. As we did so, the householder stopped us, mid retreat, with a very serious question, phrased in a deliberate and searching way, "But how did you get past the dog?" I think I said something like, "Well, he wasn't too happy but he was OK", determined not to show the man any fear or concern as I did so. We opened the door and left facing the dog again and making it back to the front gate with the snarling and lunging repeated as we did so.

Whether the gentleman came to see the film or not I don't know but God definitely protected us that day and taught us a lesson, that a mission is covered by God, however small or seemingly insignificant the mission is. Just remember, when God wants a mission carried out, He will protect it and all that are involved in it.

You know, God often allows a set of events that on their own may not seem like much but collectively, He gets His point across in a much more convincing way. The students learned a lot from the event and it started a new chapter in our thinking and in our attitudes towards trusting God.

A New Mission

Walker, a younger believer than myself, having only been 'born again' a short while before coming to the college, admitted that we had witnessed a miraculous escape that day. Was it something we shouldn't have done? Should we have been more 'wise' and used more discretion? NO. God taught us something that was priceless, that fear has to take a back seat or simply leave altogether when we decide to go the faith route. This would later be an invaluable asset at some time.

CHAPTER THREE

THE BACKWATER

Sometimes we need to retreat to a quiet place where God can get at us, where we allow Him in and let Him speak frankly to us, no holds barred. The Bible College was just one of those places. Time given to God to get away from the ideas of the world that influence us and often destroy our faith and our 'faith-thinking', is well spent. I heard and saw some great things in those days. I heard other people's life stories and saw how their lives had changed. I had time to think about what I really believed and quiet time to have my own thoughts and use my own free will, away from the former difficulties of life and time to 'get my breath', in more ways than one!

I learned more about who we are and why we are here, that is, why we are *really* here. I learned more about what we were supposed to be, not the sick, poor, feeble people the world has accepted that they are but that God had designed so much

A New Mission

more for us, with new initiatives, feelings and emotions and so much more ability than we ever realised. What God intended us to be in the beginning when He created us is far more than what we have ***devolved*** to become.

I needed a backwater and the Bible College was the start of it. I saw many miracles during my time there. We visited an evangelist's services in mid-Wales and witnessed a little girl of about 2 years of age healed of complete deafness. People say about miracles that they are 'fixed' and all just an act but this little 2 year old couldn't have acted this out. She was simply too young and I was right there and saw it all, just feet away. A lady who wore thick glasses got her sight restored to perfect that night and my friend Walker's arm, paralysed from birth, got all use and feeling back after prayer that night. These were just the boost my faith needed.

Coming back from Mid Wales one night after the students had been speaking and singing at a service there, we were a car full of five and were generally in happy mood having had a productive time in Lampeter University at their Students Christian Union. We set off for 'home' for the Bible

A New Mission

College and I made the remark, "We had better get fuel, the gauge is showing 'low' and it has a tendency to run out even when it's just nearing empty". We began looking for petrol stations and scanned the area as we drove along. I looked carefully at the fuel gauge as the needle was nearing the 'E' on the dial. On many occasions, as my garage mechanic friend and Pastor Daniel would tell you, the car ran out of fuel and he would have to come and rescue me, much to his annoyance. "Why don't you put more fuel in and keep a closer eye on it?", he would say. As a young driver though, funds were not as high as you might ideally like. Often you gambled with distances and then there was that fuel gauge that gave you the impression there was more in the tank than there was.

Anyway, we searched that Sunday night as we travelled back but fuel stations everywhere were closed. These were remote areas and this was the nineteen seventies when many garages closed on the weekend. I was getting desperate and began to worry about the situation, we had a long way to go yet, around 40 miles and what fuel I had would ***never*** get us back. I remember stopping at one

A New Mission

point and switched off the ignition in the hope that maybe the gauge had stuck and optimistically, turning the ignition key back to 'on', wished to see the needle climb and tell me things were fine. I tried it a couple of times but no change. It moved up to the 'E' but no further and I knew in my heart that this was about right, having travelled an amount of miles that made me expect that.

I turned to the students, "We had better pray if we are going to get home tonight". They all agreed and we prayed there and then. One of the students said, "Let's sing" and we began to sing and praise God for a good weekend. The miles went by and we were now way past the 'empty' stage with many miles to go. We chattered and laughed, generally stating faith things and quoting scriptures that would boost each other's faith. Looking back that was exactly the right thing to do. We had trusted God to help us, why should we despair?

The car kept going….. and going…. At one point, we reached a stage in our faith where we were saying it DARE NOT run out of fuel now! We ended up ignoring the fuel gauge and chatted and sang. The car reached landmark after landmark,

A New Mission

still we didn't give up on finding a petrol station but there were none so we drove on. Finally we reached the outskirts of the village where the Bible College was.

As we drove into the village square that night and turned the corner onto the main road that would take us to the College, the car spluttered and the engine died. I used what momentum we had to take it as far as it would go. It came to a stop at the top of a small rise just in front of the village petrol station, which was also closed. We parked the car and walked the small distance to the College.

In the morning, which was a Monday, we walked to the car and pushed it over the top of the rise and it coasted, freewheeling into the garage and it stopped a few metres short of the petrol pumps. We pushed it the remaining few metres distance and the garage attendant refuelled it. As it filled I watched the fuel gauge.

The needle took a few moments to move and then rose slowly as the fuel went in. 'So the gauge was not faulty and was working well' I thought. After

A New Mission

a few turns of the engine to pump up the fuel, the car started normally. That was a story that we all marvelled at and the students duly gave thanks to God for it.

A new pattern was emerging with my faith; the pattern was that *when we were on any kind of mission, then we had all we needed for it.*

Coming out of Bible College, I met my wife Helen and another new era in my life began. We got engaged quite soon and set plans for our wedding. My wife and I were strong in our relationship. The first time I saw her I knew this was the one. I had asked God for the right girl to marry and through all the difficulties in life, she has been dependable and although we have both had many faith challenges and needed much deliverance, God always saw us through every trial and brought us out in victory. Helen's faith, like mine, through fear and confusion on times took some odd turnings but God steered us through and we had some great victories. God is a great Father and an amazing teacher. When sickness struck, with Pneumonia attacking her many times, we stood together on God's word and promises and came

A New Mission

through in strength. With my own health, we also saw many challenges with pain and disease *but God was there* and *is still there*, **whenever we need Him**.

I think 'backwaters' give you time to get your head together. Sometimes it seems nothing is going on but all the time God keeps in touch with your thinking and development and though seemingly slow, it's sure, *if you give your life over to Him, and I can't stress that enough.* He doesn't ask a lot really because although you give over *all* of your life to Him, that life becomes more your own and a bigger and better life, a real good trade, if you want to put it that way. Along the way in our backwater, God delivered us from fear during many physically and mentally hard times.

Those times that were frightening when sickness hit, brought up many fears that God taught us to overcome and delivered us from. They ranged from fear of hospitals to fear of flying to personal fears, fear of people, fear of having too little in the bank at times to fear for our children's safety and their lives. *I want to tell you that God is way*

A New Mission

above all our fears and His peace calms ALL the storms.
Backwaters also are a development time for us to know more about what we were intended to be from the beginning. The one thing that I've learned is that **God is bigger than you think**, His abilities, His heart, His love, His initiatives, His faith, His goodness etc etc. But then, we are made in His image, His likeness and filled with His presence; *so really,* **we** *are bigger than we think too.* It follows! I'm all the time finding out about Him and how *He* thinks and it's affecting *my* thinking. As a God who is FULL of life and one who exudes health and resurrecting influences, He makes everything live that He comes in contact with. <u>We just need to catch up with that, with the Spirit of it, with the notion of it, with the LIFE of it.</u>

So many have a negative view of God. He's NOT judgemental of us, He judged Jesus instead, He's not out to get us, He's actually out to ***promote us and foster us.*** He's out to rear us well, to develop us, to make big thinkers of us and bless us. That's what His Spirit is all about, to teach us, to raise us up. But we can't always get to these things in

A New Mission

normal life. Sometimes we need to ditch the usual routines to find them out. Simply letting others do the research is not what does it. We need to touch and feel the principles to really KNOW them and see them work. Theories are often fine but doing it is a much more rewarding process and getting our hands dirty is far more of a faith producing exercise.

OK, our backwater saw us forced into situations that life threw hard at us but what we learned there was irreplaceable. We didn't want those things at the time but having to go through those experiences was the most valuable in confidence building and that confidence in God that we got, gave us great comfort for the future. He IS our 'REFUGE and OUR STRENGTH', very present with us in trouble and a great peace giver.

Now this book is entitled, 'A New Mission' and so far we haven't got to any 'Missions' in the 'Missionary abroad' sense but we have all embarked on a mission in life from birth, to make of our lives the most that we can and get to the end satisfied that we made it with good scores and happy results. Before we get to any 'Missionary'

A New Mission

adventures we mostly need preparation for them. I found that throughout my life, *God had been working hard in the background, preparing me in SO many ways, the following is a list of possible preparations that He carried out that we might all require…..*

These are not in any special order, *I needed them all :*

* Changing my attitudes
* Making me patient
* Working on my self esteem
* Developing my faith
* Giving me astounding personal stories to tell
* Creating new initiatives in me
* Building abilities in me to let me interface with others
* Giving me insight into people's needs
* Getting me to trust Him to keep me safe
* Giving me courage
* Providing me with endurance
* Getting me practical skills

The list is endless really, I was very needy as a youngster but God has that amazing ability to get

A New Mission

you what you need for a mission without you even knowing it.

Here's a good example: I remember when I was a youngster in Sunday school ….. I was always a good attendee and as they gave prizes for regular attendees. I got a book at the end of the year, presented by the Pastor and I felt duly honoured. But the books that I received year after year had a part to play in my development for missions. Dr Paul White was a missionary doctor in Africa (See, there's an African connection right there) and His books, 'The Jungle Doctor' series, told about how he tended his patients deep in the jungle. He preached the gospel to them and overcame all sorts of difficulties, making his own anaesthetic equipment, trying out new medical techniques as the need came, meeting with villagers and their tribal customs, getting by in the most adverse circumstances etc.

I think God got me hooked right there, at least in my subconscious mind. Yes it was a romantic sort of notion and a great boy's adventure story but it stayed with me. So many things attracted my mind to missions. The idea of visiting another great country of course was one, as well as all the other

A New Mission

intriguing things, the animals, the culture, the SUN! But the reality of going can also be daunting and in those backwater days and years God finds a way of equalising things in you so that you know what you are doing and are fully aware of the responsibilities before you come to making a decision that could change your life.

I SO applaud God for the way that He prepared my life for what He took me to when I first went to Africa. If I had apprehensions, He dealt with them, if I had fears, He got rid of them and took them out of the way before or during my first mission so that they would not affect His work. If I had weaknesses, then He gave me faith for every situation, and incredibly made me understand that while I was doing this for Him, I had everything I needed for the mission. I have since described the situation like this: **If God sends you on a mission, whether it's to your local town centre or the ends of the earth, He gives you a 'box' with everything you need for that mission.** In it you will find: again not in any particular order of priority: tickets, money, faith, health, food, transport, people to aid you, venues to preach at,

A New Mission

people to minister to, the words you need and the things you need for the people……. **It's a big box!**

Of course on a natural front, Bible College was a contributor in many ways to my development for missions, meeting people from other countries, being introduced to other languages on a daily basis, how to communicate and live with them, taste their foods, learn more about other cultures, even if it isn't *your* destination that they come from. We get rid of so many types of set ideas by meeting different people, even our own people, which broadens the mind. But on the spiritual front, the word of God contributed by a Bible College, puts God's nature in the forefront as something we need to know about vitally.

God's principles are the most vital. Just one word of warning though, you have to commit to God and not to religion. Religion can lead you entirely down the wrong road. That road is full of traps but the faith, life and truth road is one of great rewards. Religion is a false preparation for mission. It's a well-rehearsed set of ideas and structure that breaks down when real problems

A New Mission

arise. Faith and trust in God is a sure way because He **NEVER** lets you down.

A New Mission

> A New Mission

CHAPTER FOUR

"OUT OF THE BLUE"

"Good morning Mr Leaman", came a voice from the doorway to my office. The Headmaster stood there in His rather formal way evidently hiding someone behind him that I guessed would soon be introduced to me. "This is Mary Griffiths, she's been speaking to the children about her project in Uganda. I thought you might like to meet her". He turned about, "Mr Leaman is a Christian believer, you two might like to talk …….".

I don't remember exactly how it went but that was the gist of it. Mary sat down in my office and the conversation began, "So you're a Christian?" "Yes I'm a born again believer!", "Well that's wonderful, so am I"….. The questions flew back and fore and soon we were established.

Mary talked about her project in Africa and I was hooked straight away if I'm honest but how do these things go? I'd never been sucked into God's

56

A New Mission

purposes in such a way before, nor to such exotic purposes but that was all to come, at this point I knew nothing of what God was about to start in my life.

"We're building a Primary School in Uganda and …..". The discussion covered a broad outline of the project and it sounded interesting but in the back of my mind was another outline as God spoke to my soul. God had used me many times prophetically and in my spirit and soul something was stirring, it was almost unmistakeable. Things went from there and in time we invited Mary and her husband Alwyn down to our house in Caerphilly to talk more of it one evening. Now some while before we had come by a sum of money (around £5,000) which, we had been given by a relative but to be honest and you may find this odd, that we didn't want. There were difficult personal reasons for our decisions but we had just put it in the bank, awaiting for, well, who knows what? Then Alwyn and Mary came for the evening.

We spoke of what they were achieving in Uganda in building this school and we were very

A New Mission

impressed. My wife Helen was a Head teacher of a Primary School so it was a just right fit for her too. As the evening drew on, we heard about their challenges, to try and build more classrooms and house more pupils but funds were not easily come by. We looked at each other at one point and both disappeared into the kitchen with the same thing in our minds, to discuss what we could do.

A consensus immediately ensued as we thought of the £5,000 sitting in our bank. We went back to the lounge with a cheque for the full amount and the two burst into tears. That was one of the most rewarding things we had ever done in my mind and it was for the right reasons and the best investment, God's kingdom.

We got very interested in the King's Primary School, Bunambutye, Uganda and after a while, Mary asked, almost inevitably for me (and my soul had waited almost longingly for this question) "Why don't you come out and see the classrooms that you have built?" My heart leapt as I thought of it. Some fears rose in me too but there was a knowledge in me that this was right and the fears soon disappeared as I contemplated the

58

A New Mission

possibilities that God's purposes were going to be fulfilled in some way but I didn't know how. In the months to come, I found myself talking incessantly about it and my commitment to the project, all the time making it more and more difficult for me to back out of going to Africa, tying myself into a deal with God and chaining myself to a promise to 'go and see the school'. It was more than that though, my faith and a prophet's insight and knowledge were telling me that this was a new phase of my life beginning.

In the following February I got on a plane in Birmingham and flew to Uganda with Mary and Alwyn and we visited the school. I was really enamoured with the country and my visit. The first day there saw us, incredibly, in the Parliament building in Kampala as a guest of the then Secretary to the President, a real honour and strong link to the country. Hon. Beatrice Wabadeya was a great admirer of our project and gave us a lot of support in building the school. She invited us up to her office and security guards checked us out and required our documents and ID's. I remember sitting there in her office, next to the Presidents room, almost stunned while people talked,

A New Mission

thinking, "I wonder how many ordinary people have been privileged to sit here?"

God had opened many doors to build this school and provided many valuable resources needed for such a venture and I was impressed with what God had done. A strong link with Uganda was forming and I was being drawn in, to…. who knows what? Well God did for sure. On that first trip to the country of Uganda, when I arrived at Mbale town in the east, we visited Pearl Haven Christian Centre, a church that was Pastored by wonderful servants of God, Wilber and Sarah Okumu. They were God's own people with amazing hearts.

Both were involved with the King's Primary School to some degree. But that first Sunday morning saw us gather for morning worship at their church and I sat as a stranger to African churches but I felt very much honoured, feeling like a special guest and given a very warm welcome. That morning the Pastor got to his feet and preached his sermon. To be honest I can't remember a huge amount of his message but I do remember the main thrust of it. He had a calm but strong and deliberate approach to the message.

A New Mission

This was my first spiritual link to Uganda and God had yet to tell me what I was doing here. I knew I was here for more than just visiting a Primary school.

As the Pastor spoke, I heard more than his words, God was somehow communicating things to me that went deep inside me and I couldn't make too much sense of it. But God spoke straight into me through this man. The Pastor emphasised some points in His message. He was speaking about Moses and the children of Israel wandering in the desert. I was feeling a bit that way myself. Here I was in a strange country not knowing what I was doing here and waiting for some guidance from God about it. He came to the passage of the Bible where God gave the Israelites a pillar of fire to follow by night and a pillar of smoke by day. <u>When the pillar moved, they were to follow it, when it stayed still, they made camp.</u> Easy instructions to follow, great stuff. God was saying, "When **I** move, **you** move and keep up with me, don't run ahead of me and don't lag behind me, STAY WITH ME!" I don't know what it was about that message but it stayed right there, deep in my soul and it disturbed me, it motivated me,

A New Mission

comforted me and yet settled me, all at the same time.

We were staying at a local Hotel called the Sunrise Inn and after the service we returned there. I went to my room, deeply moved, at the point of tears from the things the Pastor had said and sat on my bed, my whole being in some sort of turmoil. I could do nothing but weep, knowing I had responsibility falling upon me but although it felt weighty, I welcomed it….. and longed for it. Confused? I certainly was. I sat on that bed and just sobbed. At that moment, Mary came into the room and seeing my state asked, "Terry, what on earth is the matter?", or words to that effect. I could hardly speak, just choking the words back but said something like, "I don't know, God's speaking to me and I don't know what to do". If I remember we prayed but some work of God had started in me that I didn't want to finish even though it was disturbing my whole being. Those words spoken by Pastor Okumu that morning stuck hard in my mind. "Don't go forward without me, don't lag behind me. **Stay with me!**"

A New Mission

As the years have passed, that message from God has been the best advice He could have given me. Had He said, "Go and do this" or "Go and do that", I might have rushed out and used my own ideas and got into many sorts of bother, speeding ahead in my own ways creating havoc as I went. But God said, *"Don't do anything without me, don't go ahead of me, move when I move"* and those words put a sensible brake on me that kept me real in everything that I did in the years to come. How sensible yet sensitive is God in His dealings with us? He knows each of us and knows how to teach us what He wants and when He wants it. He gives us good tuition and right wisdom and guidance. That is so important on a new mission where everything is fresh to us and when we are in strange territory and liable to fall foul of that strange place. But God knows what to do and keeping tight with Him keeps us safe from stupid mistakes. *I for one was so glad of God's advice.*

The rest of my time in Uganda that February was spent at the school, meeting the children, the teachers and the grounds staff and looking at what Helen and I had built with our money. There it was in bricks and mortar, making a difference in

A New Mission

around 60 or more children's lives. We had around 250 children in the school at that time, we now have 435 as this book goes to print. That was a good feeling.

As I entered one classroom, the children stood as one and welcomed us. Then they sung a song for us in their own language and I found it very emotional and I had to leave the room. When I got outside I found another man there too, also overcome by the emotional feelings of it all. This was a very moving time and it endeared me to this country and this people. I had found friends here that I didn't expect to find in a strange and different land.

God had strange ways of doing things but here I was in the thick of it and couldn't see any of it disappearing from my life any time soon. I met the villagers who greeted me enthusiastically. I visited their churches and saw their mud huts and glimpses of their home life. It was a strange new world to me and I found it hard to know what to make of it. I learned about the hazards of life in Africa, of snakes and other predators. I learned about mosquitoes and malaria, how to protect

A New Mission

myself and what water I could drink and what I couldn't and many other things. This was a lot to take in. It would take a while to know it all.

CHAPTER FIVE

FOLLOW THE PILLAR OF FIRE

I returned home to the UK and felt as though I was missing something on arriving, there was a bit missing from me that I could define easily in my own mind but wouldn't be so easy to explain to others. The next few months would be a difficult time to negotiate, trying to express to others how I felt and this at a time when I couldn't even say it to myself, "I want to return to Uganda to……". The silence in me on the subject was oddly full of all sorts of voices. The dominating one was God's still small voice, the rest were my own differing thoughts mixed with other people's comments, some good, some not so good. ***There was one certain conviction deep down inside me, I had to go back.* God would reveal why.**

Having become involved more with the Charity set up by Mary and Alwyn Griffiths, I was invited to become a Trustee of it. EZRA UK as it was named, was doing well, God sent in donations

A New Mission

miraculously and I was happy to be involved and do whatever I could to advise about the building, health and safety, hygiene etc, anything covered by my current employment remit as a Premises Manager of a large Secondary School. I was also impressed that EZRA charity used ALL of their donations well, it ALL went to the School and the children. As a Trustee, I had to pay my own way out to Uganda, we didn't take anything from funds as Trustees unlike many other charities might do. We paid our own Hotel fees, travel costs, bought our own food and paid for all sundries. This was great to me. I was sick of hearing that only tiny percentages of the funds went to the need with some large charities.

I decided that during the half term in school I would return to Uganda to the centre of Africa and I decided to go there on my own. The 'excuse' was that as a premises manager of a large school, I could be of great use there. My experience was useful in this respect and it got me on a plane that autumn to find out why I was really going there. I *did* know that I had to preach there and I remember asking God some 6 weeks or so before I flew, "Father what do I say to your people in Uganda?"

A New Mission

As I spoke I had an extraordinary experience. I had prayed so many times and asked God many questions in the past but I never expected a response in the form I got it that day. It was as though God interrupted my question, in midstream and I remember His voice drowning out my question as I was in mid sentence before I had finished asking it, ***"Tell my people, they are forgiven!"***, He said. I was stunned and a silence ensued. As I recovered myself and took a deep breath, I then said slowly, "OK Lord", I paused for a moment.... "How will that pan out?" There was no immediate answer but over the next 6 weeks up until the time I flew, God gave me an amazing message about forgiveness. I ate and slept the subject as He delivered His heart to me. My soul cried and wept at the things I heard and as the day drew near when I would fly, I felt ready, ***apprehensive but ready***.

My next question was, "Ok Lord, I have the message but where will I preach it? I know nobody in Uganda." God said nothing but it didn't faze me, I had peace about this venture. I travelled up from the capital, Kampala to the Mbale area in the east in a people carrier with a Pastor from

68

A New Mission

Uganda, Pastor Michael Mandali. We talked about God and spoke for quite a while about how we became Christians and our family backgrounds etc., generally acquainting each other with our personal situations and during a very short lull in the conversation, Michael looked straight at me. He had a very deliberate turn of phrase as he pointed at me and said, ***"You have to preach in Uganda!"*** I said, "Yes I know, I have the message". Then he said to me, ***"And I have all the places where you will preach".***

God had just opened His missions box and in it were all the things I needed and I was just learning the lesson of it as I went. By the end of that first week, on my own in Uganda, I was speaking to a crowd of around 2,500 in the local football stadium in Mbale. Talk about being thrown in at the deep end! These were born again believers all gathered for a nightlong prayer meeting in the pitch dark. They had a crude speaking platform set up made of rough wood illuminated by a string of light bulbs over the top of it.

"But these are all born again Father and I have a gospel message of forgiveness", my heart said.

A New Mission

But nevertheless I preached the message God had given me. I got on my feet at about 10:30pm and finished about 11:45pm speaking through an interpreter in the pitch dark and when I asked for a response from the people, 38 flocked around the makeshift platform to give their lives to Jesus.

No one was more surprised than me really. I don't know why, the prophet in me told me this was right being here and delivering this message was right too but it still shook me. I had just seen God do something with me I had never seen before. Oh people had got saved when I had preached before, people had been healed as I prophesied and preached on some occasions but this was a shock to my system and what a lovely shock! I asked the local Pastors wife, "Will you follow up with these people?" I was concerned that now they were born again, they would need support in their new lives. "Oh yes, we have their names and addresses!" she replied. God had everything covered.

On the following Sunday morning, Michael said, "Today you are speaking to a school assembly at 9 am and then at 11 am you speak to the Miracle

A New Mission

Faith Church just a short walk away from the school".

I again preached 'forgiveness' to a packed school assembly of over 200 pupils with a great anointing of God's Spirit on the message and at the end asked all the pupils in this secondary school to stand with me and pray. I prayed and put all these lovely young people into God's hands for His guidance and placed them into His care, that He would change them and in so doing, change their lives. Because I had to rush away from the school and be at the next venue to preach at eleven, I left it at that.

When I got home from Uganda I got an email from the Principal of the school, Pastor John Were. It read, "When you left after the school assembly, we felt this was such a powerful message that you preached, we felt to make an appeal for those who wanted salvation and I have to tell you that the whole school responded in giving their lives to Jesus. **I can't tell you what that message did to me.** My heart almost stood still when I read it and tears welled in my eyes. There was a stillness about the moment as my faculties tried to come to

A New Mission

terms with the email. How do you respond when news like that comes? God had just done the totally unexpected, again I don't know why it was unexpected, God had planned it all and He doesn't do anything by halves but everything He does just works and I knew that but it was still a surprise. A wonderful surprise! All these things confirmed to me that Uganda was going to be a special place in my life.

As I stated earlier, I was due to speak at another Church in Kampala at 11am that day after speaking at the school where all these young people received salvation. I hurried on foot to the Church, arriving there just before 11am. We set up my radio microphone and I spoke to the Pastor who questioned me more closely about my 'Professional' credentials and about 'my Church'. I told him I was not a Pastor and had no church and this really bothered him. It seemed he wanted only 'qualified' clergy speaking at his church. At that time I was not recognised as a Pastor in Uganda, as I am today. I was however the Editor of an online Christian faith magazine called 'The Overcomer' and God said, "Tell him about it", which I did. That seemed to satisfy him to some

A New Mission

degree. I had been well recommended to him and his church so I wondered what his problem was. He then quizzed me as to what I would speak about and I informed him I would speak about forgiveness, the message God gave me for Uganda. His response was, "There's no point, all these here today are born again". I said, "Well that's what God has told me" and stuck to my convictions.

He agreed to let me speak and then tried to control it by setting the time limit on my sermon by giving me just 30 minutes to speak through an interpreter, which was not enough time to discharge the whole message. I heard God whisper in my ear, 'Just go ahead but include the Pastor in the message'. As I got up to speak, determined to preach all of the message, which would take around an hour, I occasionally turned and looked at the Pastor and directed many of my thoughts in his direction, smiling as I did. It appeared that he forgot all about the clock and my time limit so I carried on to the end. I finished about an hour or more later and gave an appeal that if any wanted salvation and forgiveness of sin, to come forwards. Around 20 responded and came to the front to make Jesus

A New Mission

their Saviour and Lord. At this, the Pastor got up and addressed the congregation in a severe voice, "God spoke **this exact message** to you 2 weeks ago and I cannot help feeling He is speaking to you again today and more of you need to repent!" As he spoke 2 more came forwards, sobbing and weeping their way to the Lord.

In all, 22 received salvation that Sunday morning. It was a good job that I ignored what the Pastor had told me. God had already given the message He wanted spoken to **'His' people** and that message brought the response from **His people's hearts.** I was so relieved to know that the voice I had followed was His voice and not my own sometimes unsure and doubtful thoughts. It taught me a great lesson to always follow God's voice and direction *and not to move without Him.*

A new ministry was forming in me. That evening I spoke the same message to a church in the slum area of Kampala and everyone, even the Pastor's wife came forward for forgiveness and salvation. What an amazing start to my ministry in Uganda.

A New Mission

Over 300 came to Jesus on that trip and responded to the message that God told me to deliver, in less than a week.

I decided that I could not ignore the events of that trip into Africa and the following year decided to return again and minister wherever God, through Pastor Mandali, would take me. The call had indeed come 'out of the blue' through an encounter in school with Mary and a conviction that God had firmly planted in me, over many years. It had started way back when I was a child and suddenly it had formed miraculously into a firm ministry that was changing lives. Did I have a lot to do with it? It felt not, it seemed that God had pulled together so many preformed things in my earlier life and made a masterpiece of it for His Glory. **Amazing! God is just amazing!**

CHAPTER SIX

DO IT AGAIN LORD!

Pastor Mandali was such an asset to my trips to Uganda. For my second visit, the following year, he arranged ministry in many different places. I don't know how he was led to take me to go those locations, I never asked. All I know is that everywhere we went people listened intently to the word of God and many got saved and some got healed or set free. After the plane touched down in Entebbe we travelled to Kampala and then on to Mbale town. I had an invitation from Pastor Okumu to speak at his Living Waters Church on the Sunday morning. I was very honoured. This man has a great ministry, I just prayed that I could fill his shoes that morning. But this is something else that I had to learn 'on mission', that I now had to go to places and fill the shoes of Pastors and men of God that I looked up to and preach in places that I had no prior information about.

A New Mission

There would be places I would preach where there were large congregations of over a thousand and where faith was already alive and well. How would I 'perform' in those circumstances? And there you have it…. This was not a performance, neither should I be trying to fill some other minister's shoes who had a great ministry. God was beginning to teach and confirm to me that what He had given me was precise and 'made for purpose'. What I had was unique to me just as much as to those I looked up to had unique ministries.

As I looked back over my life, I saw some unique things that not many had experienced and whenever I gave testimony to those things that God had done in my life, people were often mesmerised and I saw their faith lifted in a way I hadn't seen before. I decided to use my life story more in preaching and see where it went because what these 'missions' were all about was getting publicity, as it were, for the gospel of Jesus Christ.

The more I told of what God had done in my life, the more it changed people's lives, more people gave their lives to God and more people got healed

A New Mission

and set free from their problems. *Let me tell you something, the most powerful thing you have to tell is that of what God did in your life.* God gave it to me this way: when the word (Jesus) became flesh and dwelt among us, we beheld His glory. When the word becomes flesh in *you*, when **His word** happens in *your life*, His glory will be seen again - it's the 'God evidence' in your life that shows who and what He is.

My confidence in my own delivery of what I had, was growing and soon fears started to leave me and I saw my faith grow further as they left. So I stepped into 'pulpits' I wouldn't have had the courage to try and fill before. God was teaching me again, that His 'Missions box' contained a lot more than I had realised. God was telling me that **I** was what he had prepared for this work, not reputations or qualifications for the role or being a big name speaker but plain and simply, *me*. *That was hard to swallow for me.* I had lots of things in my background that told me that I was behind all the others when it came to confidence. My problems with my set backs in schooling and poor health had seen to that. This was the lad who couldn't run because of Asthma, who couldn't

A New Mission

keep up in school because of being a class behind everyone else but God was starting to tell me differently. He was giving me a new confidence in who *I* was; this time it was based on a different set of criteria. I was beginning to see that our 'new creation' had another set of abilities and these were far more valuable than any of the others I had considered to be important in life.

As I continued to minister around Uganda, I noticed that my (I.E., God's) message was having a different impact. People didn't consider me incapable, instead they were keen to have me speak and showed all the signs of having their faith increased when I preached and they started believing for things they needed. You can think that these 'confidence' things didn't matter but they did, with my background they were very relevant and as usual, God dealt with them all. His 'Missions Box' was full of all the stuff I needed.

My next call that year was to visit the Kings Primary School and I carried out a report of the building, the curriculum, the grounds, the state of the toilets etc and I bought them anything I could to advance things. I bought medicines, emergency

A New Mission

Malaria treatments, a new wheelbarrow, footballs, some mosquito nets for the huts in the village etc. I went around the village finding recruits for the next school year with Beatrice Simeo, one of our board members and the local village Pastor's wife (and also a great interpreter for me when I spoke there) and the ever attendant Pastor Michael Mandali. God had sent this man and he was a great blessing.

I had other duties to perform in those days too. Sometimes there were discipline matters at the school when teachers or the Headteacher were not performing well or they had caused problems. As the one 'going out to Uganda' at that time, it often fell to me to investigate things and sometimes to dismiss staff. I felt like 'The Terminator' on occasions but it was part of the school's development and needed to be done, to dismiss them and employ better.

The school has been a great 'vision' from God. Mary and Alwyn stepped out in faith to provide it and God came through for the project. It was so obviously a miracle school. Anyone who doesn't hold that view hasn't looked closely enough at

A New Mission

what has been done. At every turn God sent the finance and provided all sorts of things that we needed. I believe it has touched many more lives than we realise and will continue doing so. The children alone have had their lives dramatically altered by the school's existence, let alone the effect on the local village who now have fresh water and their own fine school that has already given hope to many generations. Following the installation of the water bore hole that goes down deep in the ground and pulls up fresh water, many fatal diseases disappeared quickly from the village and area, so this alone has changed so many lives there.

When we hear God's voice and do what He says, His people get better lives and we get a portion of the blessing. We now have a goat and cattle breeding programme in the village where the people get free cattle and goats to increase the wealth of the area. We also have 3 new churches and buildings that can be used for many purposes in the north, middle and south of the village. God's legacy to us is a good one. But the main reasons for my excursions to Uganda cannot be forgotten. As I see it, God's heart is to save His

A New Mission

people and to save **all** of His people. While the ministry of the school to the village of Bunambutye and in particular the children of the area is a huge one and is making a massive difference to their welfare and education, there is a bigger ministry being carried out that Mary's 'vision' of building the school also provided, as part of God's plan. We need to remember that I went to Uganda because of the school and all the extra ministries that exist now, came out of that first vision. As we establish churches there and bring God's word to the people, there is a growth of faith and the life of God is established both there in Bunambutye village and around Uganda.

I've been very encouraged by seeing new thinking springing out of people's faith. The lack of initiative that fear and doubt creates has a big effect on the faith of the people. One thing I have witnessed that has amazed me, is that as I have preached faith and raised the expectancy of men and women, children too, I have seen life fill up their faces and it provoked their voices into praise to God. I have perceived that whereas there was no praise or joy before and people struggled to raise their thoughts above their problems and

A New Mission

issues, faith has the opposite effect of creating a new attitude and lifts the personality to new heights of hope in all situations.

As I've visited Uganda and waited on God year after year for 'the message' He wants delivered, He has given me specific things to say and I've watched the operation of His Spirit in the people. Every year people have got saved and healed with many miracles happening around Uganda. One of the recurring events is that as I preach, often people tell me later, "As you preached today, God took away my pain" or, 'this happened, or that happened'. One of my drivers who drove me around Uganda one year, asked me as we talked in the car one day to pray for him. As we drove along he explained that he wanted to follow the Lord more closely and felt he needed prayer, so I put my hand on him as he drove and discharged what was in my heart on the matter. As we drove along, he said to me, "We need another service in my own neighbourhood in Kampala, could we have one on Saturday evening?" I referred him to Pastor Michael Mandali who organises my itinerary. Michael said, "Ok we will arrange it!"

A New Mission

On the Saturday evening we squeezed yet another service into our tight schedule and when the evening arrived, I got up to preach. The young man arrived a little late for the meeting but was very interested in all that I said. He came up to me afterwards and made a confession to me, "I was a little late this evening because I have been racked in pain all day, I had such a bad headache I couldn't concentrate at all, it was almost closing my eyes". He went on… "but as you preached all the pain disappeared and I now have no pain at all!"

We don't always see healings in every service but we do very often witness some great events when pains go and cancer is healed or people who have had a stroke get healed and we witness great events where people at the point of death get great strength and life. Often though, as we move on, a phone call comes and we are told of another healing or event. All across Uganda I have seen the word of God save souls and heal people, create new faith, destroy fear, give peace and change lives. Most recently in Kigali Rwanda I saw many in a congregation getting release from fear, including a Pastor. I saw release come to Him and

A New Mission

got a witness in my spirit that fear had left him. He spoke to me afterwards and gave me a great hug and gripped me really tightly, not letting me go for quite a while. He sobbed and said, "I felt fear leave me". I said quietly in his ear, "I know... I saw it go. Praise God!" The word of God had moved the congregation and I saw them realise who they are, and it changed them. They simply rejoiced from deep down as God spoke into them. All this developed out of Mary's initial vision.

I have no agenda but God evidently does. My 'mission' and that's a good word for it, is to listen to God and deliver what He gives me, to the people. He knows their hearts and what is going on in their lives. I may have never met them before but God knows them intimately. What amazed me year after year, is that it happened again and again. For God to do it once was miraculous to me. To make something great happen like He did, for hundreds to get saved and see all those lives changed was one thing, that was a single great event but to see another event occur in another part of the country and even more born again and healed is sometimes hard to follow in your mind.

CHAPTER SEVEN

A WIDENING MISSION

The next few years saw my 'missions' go deeper into Uganda as Pastor Michael took me further into different countryside. As soon as my school report was complete, we set off travelling northwest and then south, crossing the equator. I remember the odd feeling as I stood under the sign saying 'Equator' marked by a steel plate coming out of the ground and disappearing back into it. It was a nice touch and I'm sure many thought that it was actually a tangibly real thing like that. We saw large townships, remote villages and then the car climbed into mountainous areas. We saw so many landscapes, beautiful scenes I had never imagined. We travelled south to Mount Rwenzori and Fort Portal, ascending up onto volcanic landscapes where there were salt lakes and lava rock formations, elephant grass and all sorts of wildlife. As we travelled, baboons sat by the side of the road in places just waiting for travellers to stop and toss them food. Some carried babies on their

A New Mission

underside, properly called 'infants', like human children and we were warned not to bother them as they could become aggressive.

You really needed a guide when travelling in those areas, at least someone from the country to notify you of the dangerous things. Michael Mandali was everything of this, a great liaison in all matters, how and where to buy stuff, how the Ugandan system worked, whether the traders were ripping you off, sorry….., taking advantage of your 'ignorance' of the normal prices. As soon as a white face would appear there was a propensity shall I say, for prices to rise. By how much often depended on many factors, whether you look suitably ignorant of the ways of the country or whether your dress is smart and affluent, or if you happened to pull a wad of notes out of your pocket when you went to buy something (the currency meant you had a lot of notes in your pocket, often amounting to hundreds of thousands of Ugandan Shillings), all of these had a bearing on the situation. Most of the time these days, I keep out of sight in the vehicle and let Michael or my driver do the shopping. Stuff often costs half the price that way. You many not consider that too much

A New Mission

but on a mission we have a budget that most of us have to adhere to closely.

Up on Mount Rwenzori that year, the mountain range in the South Western region of Uganda, we held a 3 day convention in a village church right on the top. I was amused to find that I was the first white minister to preach there. Always as I travel around I hear the word 'Mzungu' which is the term 'White man'. Travelling through a town or village, you will sometimes hear the children shout it. If you are sensitive about things like that, missions may not be for you. It's not usually derogatory but it does single you out. I'm often aware that sometimes I'm the only white person in town and often the focus of attention. In big towns not so much but in small villages, people will talk about you and 'be curious' shall I say and often the Mzungu word appears again. I've had children come up to me and feel my arm to see if it feels like theirs, never having seen a white man before.

While on top of this mountain range I was also very surprised and humbled to find that many of the congregation had walked over 6 miles to get there. It was quite a climb in our vehicle but these

A New Mission

people came on foot. They sang and danced their praises to the Lord in the services and were obviously uplifted by the word. Many got born again and healed. It was uplifting to see young people kneeling, accepting Jesus as their saviour.

To my surprise again, because Africa is full of surprises, the Pastor kept rabbits. He took me around to the rear of their house and there among the banana trees, the mangos and cassava plants, he showed me crude hutches he had made and inside them were black and white rabbits, like I had as a pet when a child. They were recognisably the 'Black and White Dutch' breed, they were unmistakeable. I asked why he kept them, silly question really, he pointed to his open mouth and made a chewing movement. I tried not to think of the pet I once had as he did so. I was relieved to find that the meal we had that day was rice, cassava, beans and ...... chicken.

Beautiful landscapes were not what I thought Uganda was going to be about. I had come for one thing, to bring a Father's message to His people, His children. How fitting to do it in the beautiful world He had created. These things make you

A New Mission

reconsider many things, not least all **of, who you are** and that brought a new revelation to me. Away from my normal environment I was forced to think differently and see things with a new perspective. ***Everyone***, I thought, should come on a mission, it changes you, you're never the same again. That was a nice time, like God had rewarded me personally for the long trek from the UK and for my obedience to His directions. I didn't arrange it this way but God blessed me this way.

We stayed in a villa on the mountain slopes and the landscape was almost Swiss in appearance on occasions with alpine flowers in a meadow and on the far hill, black and white Freesian cows were grazing, while down in the base of the valley was a lake, in which, I was told, were crocodiles. Now there's a combination you don't get every day.

But this is about mission and the packed church, day after day saw the word of God opened up and faces glowed with new life as God revealed Himself. For me, a mission is all about what we don't know, that we need to know, that God will reveal to us that will make swinging changes to

A New Mission

our lives, through the life of His Spirit. Speaking to the nations about our redemption is meant to impart more than having our sins forgiven, it's about revealing to people who they are now and what they can expect from this new life and what their new creation is all about after they get born again and it always surprises me what God does in people once they realise who they are.

A **w i d e n i n g** mission is not just going to new places, though that certainly happened but **becoming a BIGGER person** is what God is after. Having a bigger heart for His people, preaching a bigger message because you have a bigger vision of who God is, makes you end up well...., **bigger**.

A New Mission

Chapter Eight

A HICCUP IN THE MISSION?

At the last minute, as I arrived in Uganda in September 2010, Michael asked if I could speak at an evening Prayer Meeting ("That's different". I thought!). We were in the Capital City, Kampala and I was due to speak at a Secondary School Valedictory Service at their end of school celebration the next day, which was a Saturday. We arrived at the Miracle Faith Church in Nsambya, Kampala at around 7 pm. I preached a message of faith that night, that, 'With God all things are possible' and the entire church stood with me in rededication to God and the vision of faith. There was a great atmosphere there. God had moved the congregation without a doubt. I hadn't expected such a response and it was a great start to the mission.

As I stepped out into the dark that night, because in September it's pitch black at night at that time, we had around 500 metres to walk to get to the

A New Mission

villa where I was staying. The street lighting in the area is almost non-existent even though it's a suburb of the capital of Uganda. We walked around 40 metres or so, crossed a road and then stepped onto the pavement on the opposite side of the road. As I placed my left foot down to where I thought the pavement was still running, my foot went into a culvert and landed on the steep-angled side of it. There was an excruciating pain as my foot twisted and rolled onto its side and then continued rotating as the full weight of my body came down on it. I immediately yelled out and as I felt the awful pain, along with it came a sensation that my shoe was suddenly getting very tight, as though the shoe was getting smaller. In fact, my foot was rapidly swelling and the pain level was increasing with the growth. I began to feel faint and as I hopped on one foot to stabilise myself, Pastor Mandali grabbed me and steadied me in the pitch dark to keep me upright.

I stooped down and gripped my ankle with one hand and put my other hand in the air, reaching up as it were for the Almighty's help. I heard myself saying, "In Jesus Name Father, help me".

A New Mission

A few metres away was a shop with a dim glow coming from the doorway and we made straight for it, with Michael trying to shuffle me across to a seat in front of it. As I reached the crude bench, I slumped onto it, trying to get my breath after it had been knocked out of me with the shock of the pain. I called out to God and we prayed aloud, ignoring all else that was going on around us.

I've no idea what the people around us thought, it was irrelevant. My instinct was to try and get back to the villa as soon as possible. My feeling was that I had broken my ankle or done serious damage to my foot. Having done a lot of medical first aid training in industry, I knew all about limb damage and knew these symptoms well. As we moved across to the pavement again, to try and get back to the villa, the faintness came over me again. We stopped, having reached the pavement; it was very hard to move forward, even with Michael taking my weight on the injured side. So we stayed there on the side of the road and prayed again.

Michael was obviously very concerned and I was trying to compose myself. We prayed in the Holy Spirit in unknown tongues for a minute or two

A New Mission

until it was difficult to hold me up any longer. After we had prayed, I felt no changes in my foot but there *was* an alteration in my confidence level, I suddenly felt strength come into my mind. Michael said, "Let me go and see if I can get my friend who is a doctor, you may have to go to hospital." That last statement was one too far for me. I said, "Michael, I don't have the time to go to hospital, I have to preach for the next 3 weeks, it's why I'm here. I have no time to go to hospital." Now that may seem like an odd thing to say but that's how I saw the situation.

That's how my faith seemed to be saying it to me, there was simply too much to do and I had come 4,500 + miles to do it, at some expense and that just backed up my attitude. I made a decision. I said to Michael, "Let's get to the Villa and put this foot up." We switched on the lights on our mobile phones and lit up the pathway. I went hopping and shifting on one foot on Michael's arm and we made our way along the rough mud surface of the side street for around 500 metres until we finally reached 'home'.

A New Mission

Once inside, I took my shoe off and we saw the damage. I have always described my damaged foot this way, whether because I was in Africa or just because it was the best description, 'as looking as it was', 'like an elephant's foot'. The swelling was really big and I was so relieved to get my shoe off. They brought me ice to put on it but it was very painful to bear. Michael said to me, "Let's pray again" and I agreed willingly because that was what my spirit was already saying. Then a lad around 16 years of age from the villa called Paul came into the room. I called him over and said, "Come on Paul, pray with us". We laid hands on the foot and prayed. The lad prayed lovely, and Michael and myself joined together with him with faith rising high in our beings.

It was a short but firm prayer, no holds barred. We told our common enemy that he had no dominion over us and released the power of the Holy Spirit into the situation. As we finished that short prayer, we looked at the foot again and before our eyes, the swelling visibly went down really quickly. I felt some real immediate relief and rested my foot adding the ice to it to consolidate what had already happened. People fussed over me for half an hour

A New Mission

or so until they were convinced that I was stable and settled, getting me drinks and cushions and I then thanked them and told them to go back to their families and their beds. I settled in for the night, taking some Paracetamol to help me sleep and got into bed. It became an unexpectedly quiet night, not like the way it had started out.

In the morning, I rose from my bed gingerly and for a while didn't put any weight on my foot. There was a lot of bruising but there seemed to be hardly *any* swelling left and after a while I thought to put a little weight on it. To my surprise I found it was quite robust, with little or no pain. So I stood up and leaned on that side. It didn't hurt, so I put more and more weight on it. It held all my weight with no pain, nothing appreciable at any rate. As the morning ensued, people fussed again but were amazed at my recovery. The severe bruising was a real testimony to what had occurred the night before. It looked like a black sock on my foot and even extended underneath the foot. There was also yellow bruising up my leg as far as the calf muscle. People looked at me in disbelief as I placed all my weight on the foot. When I softly stamped my foot on the floor, they couldn't

A New Mission

believe it and looked stressed, wincing as I did so. "And you have no pain?" they said. "No", I replied without any sign of a wince myself. They still fussed over me though.

The next day I spoke at the school valedictory service and testified about the previous evening's experience. They were mesmerised at the story and it was the highlight of the day as I showed them the bruising. Three days later I was buying Emergency Malaria packs for the village of Bunambutye in a pharmacy in Mbale town. As I stood at the counter, my foot felt a little stiff and asked the pharmacist if he had an ointment or gel for it, to help it loosen up a bit. "Let me see it", he said. I removed my shoe and sock. "My word" he said, "are you in a lot of pain?" I said "No, none". "When did you do it?" "Friday" I said. "Which Friday?" He asked. "Last Friday", I said. He just looked at me and said, "I can't believe it." So I told him the whole story. It turned out he was a Christian believer from Pastor Okumu's church and again it made an impact when I preached there. Well if these things happen, I make sure God gets the glory from the situation. That way

A New Mission

the negative takes a back seat and maybe Satan thinks twice about trying to afflict me again.

As the mission progressed, I decided to begin every sermon with my testimony about the foot being healed. Pastor Michael commented that the message was particularly powerful this year and the responses from congregations were amazing, then added, "Do you know what's really making them step up their faith? It's your foot testimony. They are amazed." I took the liberty in a few churches to remove my shoe and sock to lend proof to the story and it just lifted the roof.

We can wonder about why God would let this happen to me, as if it were His fault I didn't see the culvert and hurt myself but really, I am so glad it happened. I got a great testimony out of it, God got the glory and many had a faith lift. Everyone got blessed. Great! Part of my 'mission' came about this way. We can panic at the time, I could have gone the usual route and got hospital treatment, laid up in bed etc., but the mission was what I was there for and somehow that's what the Holy Spirit showed me. The bottom line is, God brought me this way, fixed the foot, made

A New Mission

everything good and the mission went on. It IS about the mission. So, a hiccup in God's planning? No. So did God plan the damage to my foot? No. Did God recover the situation after I damaged myself? Yes. Was the mission a failure? No. Was the mission turned into a better situation? Yes. Would I trust God to take me on another mission? **Absolutely.**

A New Mission

> A New Mission

CHAPTER NINE

PROVIDING HELP

It wouldn't be right to leave out a section about what can naturally be done for the people of a country. Knowing what help is needed in Areas like Uganda is quite an important aspect of what we have always done there. Providing a school is a HUGE help to a country like Uganda. Providing a quality school much better than what they have at present is an even better help. The plan was to provide a school to more or less British Standards remembering of course that the school is remote from Britain and there are other factors such as the curriculum used in Uganda and that these are Ugandan children who have a very different background to our own.

On a mission you have to always remember the background of the people you are ministering to. Simply ignoring their culture and doing what you think, is not viable or proper. But any aid given to the people of another country such as Uganda must

A New Mission

be purely helpful to them with no thoughts of changing their culture to make it the same as your own. Naturally the gospel will change lives. Of course there are so many things they would like from our culture *but this is not a take-over, this is help.*

Apart from providing a school, which is a huge undertaking, we tried taking out many things for people, like clothes, mobile phones, spectacles, medicines, laptop computers etc in suitcases at every trip but then realised there were probably better things to give them and many things are cheaper and more suited to their purpose than some of the things we could buy in the UK and cheaper to buy in Uganda too. One thing in particular is medicines. Malaria medicine is easily available there and much cheaper than if you buy it in the UK. We buy emergency packs of 'Courtem' for example, a brand of treatment designed for treating Malaria on a 3 day basis to overcome the quick onslaught of the disease. This is a much more 'on the ground' medicine and does the job well and is cheaper to buy in Uganda. It may also be illegal to take in medicines from another country. they could need an import licence or be

A New Mission

passed by the country's health system for use there. Also more recently we are finding that Uganda has made more provision for its people by setting up local clinics in many areas. There may be remote places that don't have this yet and of course that's where we can help but often medicine is available there now.

Wondering what we could do to help villagers I asked one of our school employees who was acting as a premises manager for us there at the time, "Deo, what can we do for the village that could be a real help to them?" He replied, "Give me a day or two to think of what could be the best and most practical!" I liked that reply because most people will pick a quick answer and define goods that tickle their fancy and often this can be expensive and ineffective. Deo Mushembe came back to me the next day with a great answer. He said, "You know, many don't have a hoe for digging, if they had one it would really help." I spoke to my driver Rashid who lived in Mbale town and asked him where I could buy hoes and how much they would be. "I could buy them for you at wholesale price in boxes of 24, if you would like", he said, "They would be much cheaper". They turned out to be a

A New Mission

good price, around £2:70 each which includes a hardwood handle so we bought 24 at a time and they were great quality and strong. In fact when I came home that year I bought one for my garden because they are much better to use than a British spade.

Of course we are talking about missions so our next revelation was to bless villages after we had ministered God's word there. We didn't tell churches we were going to do anything like this but after the service, we announced that we had a gift for them and it brought huge elation from the congregation. I have rarely seen such excitement from people. They sang, danced and screamed even with delight. I would never have believed that such small gifts would bring such a reaction. It is now one of our main aids to villages. The immediate change to agriculture in a village is amazing. If you give them tools of any kind, they straightway start using them to better their lives. Of course, African hoes are not just used for agriculture. They use them for making bricks, digging foundations, to provide irrigation and digging trenches and generally build their houses with them. A small cost but a big investment in

A New Mission

the people's lives. An additional gift of seeds to the village, for planting, is a great compliment to the hoe programme. In our last trip we gave out around 150 hoes. That has made a difference to around 150 families.

As an additional feature to this programme and remembering this is a mission scenario, we speak to each church and say that this is a gift from the church in the UK to them (which brings great euphoria and a lovely reaction) to their village. If any family does not have a hoe, we advise the church to give them one, whether they are Christian or not, whether Muslim or whoever they are.

This venture is to bring glory to God, which is why we present things to the local church elders. The gift of a hoe or seeds to villagers are then seen as coming from God. After visiting one church, Rashid, my driver, who is a Muslim, asked me if he should get the hoes and seeds out of the car boot. I use a Muslim to drive me sometimes because he gets to see what we do and hear what we preach. I said, "Yes, thank you Rashid, I had forgotten!" He disappeared to the car and carried

A New Mission

the items out and put them on the grass in front of the Pastor. As the Pastor received them and was looking at them, Rashid asked me, "Are these for the Christians only?" I replied, "No Rashid, these are for anyone who doesn't have a hoe, whether they are Christians, non-believers, Muslims or whoever." At this he got very excited, shaking a little and his eyes welled up and he said, "Maybe they will be born again now!" What we do, when it is from God's heart affects everyone around and they **all** see who God really is.

We have done the same thing in buying goats for villages. We try to buy goats that are pregnant and when the kids are born and weaned, we ask recipients of the goats to give a kid away to those who have none, which endears the community to the church and promotes God's love between villagers. I always remember a lady coming into the service who was dressed differently to the other ladies and after sitting through the service she announced that she had come to the service to thank me because she had received a goat. She too was a Muslim. What a great response and how endearing to the church and a great message to people that we are all Gods children.

A New Mission

There are now goat breeding programmes going on and people are sharing their goats. The same has happened with cows. We bought cows for villages and they have bred, so more people now have a cow in their family. They get more fresh milk as a product and also breed cows to give away. Cattle are a sign of prosperity and status in the villages, it's good that it is seen to come from God's hand. It didn't come from my hand, it was God's idea!

Mosquito nets were an early venture to give away to households. To protect the family from malaria mosquitoes was easy and quite cheap. A net is quite low cost but if it's large enough for the family to sleep under and many fit the inside of a traditional round grass or tin roofed hut easily, it protects them all.

I always take clothes on a mission to give away. Any spare room in a suitcase can be used to take them and most churches in the UK have spare good clothes to give away. I usually insist on new items complete with labels or at least hardly worn clothes. There's little point giving clothes that have only half the wear left in them, and it doesn't say so much about the gift itself if we give things

A New Mission

that we have finished with. Deo Mushembe also had an initiative to provide villagers with tools. As an extension to this, he suggested a village tool store. In this way, if anyone needed to borrow a tool, they could collect it from the church. This means people can get on with learning building skills as well as making homes. Sometimes a village carpenter can give lessons too. We try to provide particular help, when we have the funds that often our home church members or churches provide as gifts for the mission.

Recently we have provided new roofs for Ugandan churches, cement for building, sewing machines for providing work for mothers, Microphones for the bigger churches sound systems etc.

There are no set rules as to what we provide. Whatever God sends, we take and there's always a niche somewhere for it to fit. One church was expanding as a result of our missions there. The Pastor, who had suffered a stroke had asked if I would go to the home to pray for him. When I went to the home, he was confined to bed and the signs of a severe stroke were all over him. His face had dropped on his left side, His left arm and left

A New Mission

leg were also paralysed. He couldn't get out of bed and the church was diminishing as a result. I put my hand on him and prayed for healing in the name of Jesus. A year later I returned to the same church in Busia village in the east of Uganda and they introduced me to a man that I didn't really recognise. It was the Pastor I had prayed for. He got up in the church to tell his story of how he started to get better immediately after we had prayed. I looked at him and there were no signs of any stroke. He walked ok, he talked ok, his face was normal again and his left arm and leg functioned properly. The bit I liked was that after he got healed, his ministry became more powerful and the church is now expanding.

They had all the bricks there at the back of the church ready to extend the building. As one of our further gifts to the church, we left them with enough money to buy the cement for the extension.

So the missions have taken on new aspects as the Lord has revealed to us what to do. Providing anything that you can, may be such a help to Churches and this helps spread the Gospel. For example I had a spare lighting mixer at home. It

A New Mission

was an L.E.D lighting (DMX) controller capable of running up to 256 different LED lighting units. I took it out to Uganda and it is now used in one of the biggest churches in Mbale town, a 3,000 seat capacity church, which is rapidly becoming finished, a powerhouse of Gospel ministry. We have supplied microphones and anything people give us as gifts to churches there.

I wish I had more desks, furniture and another container-load of things for the school in Bunambutye as we have taken there before because my vision is that one-day we will have a Secondary School there as well. The 435 or more children in the Kings Primary School will need Secondary education when they leave but the God who built the Primary School will I'm sure, keep providing until all the children's needs are met.

I'm seeing a 'MISSION' as more than just 'an important task that someone is sent to do', as the dictionary puts it. To many it is vital, to more it is imperative. People somewhere are hurting emotionally, others are physically sick, some need new life - the born again sort that preachers deliver from God when they preach. Others need peace,

A New Mission

or joy or love or the ability to love. God can deliver those things if we are prepared to go on a mission. It doesn't have to be abroad, it can be a mission to a neighbour or to a town or to a family. So many people need a mission. It doesn't have to look like you are on a mission when you do it, it can be plain, ordinary help. Alcoholics, addicts, old people, young people, the middle aged, the well and the infirmed, all waiting for God to intervene in their difficult lives. Wherever there's a need, a mission can be launched.

Before I end this chapter, I want to make a special point of giving my sincere thanks and express my deep appreciation to the people of Victory Church in Cwmbran UK, to friends, family and all those who have given generously to ensure that I never go to Uganda empty handed but have given so kindly large amounts of funds, far more than I could have ever expected to provide such lovely things for the people of Uganda. In addition I want to pay tribute especially too to the donors to EZRA Trust UK Charity who have given faithfully over the years to build the Kings Primary School and educate our children. May God

A New Mission

further raise up donors to carry out the rest of the mission that is the Kings Primary School and the village of Bunambutye. May God's Richest Blessings be yours and to all that provide for God's children, however old they are or wherever thy live! Thank you so much.

CHAPTER TEN

A MISSIONS FULL PURPOSE

The unmistakeable and most powerful of purposes of any mission going anywhere is to change lives for the better. The Gospel of Jesus Christ is the most powerful message because it DOES just that, it changes lives. I've seen thousands of people born again on a single mission, I've seen people physically healed, emotions repaired and miracles of many types. To me the definition of preaching a 'full gospel' is seeing the signs and wonders following the preaching of God's word. Let's look at that for a moment. The command of Jesus to the disciples in Mark 16 after His resurrection was, "Go into all the world and preach the gospel to every creature". It's interesting that this command came after the resurrection. The resurrection is an event where someone lifeless was made alive again after the visitation to the tomb by the Holy Spirit. I love to think of this in the context of a mission.

A New Mission

If God made us in His image, His likeness and filled us with His presence, His Spirit, in other words we are made tri-partite exactly like Himself, and then God gave man dominion (the ability to dominate or rule the whole earth in peace) such that nothing should dominate man at all. Then in giving man a free will, why then should man be dictated to in any way? God is all powerful (omnipotent) and nothing rules Him, so having a free will is part of His natural being of not having anything rule over Him. When He made man, that freedom of will was a natural inheritance to man. When however man gave in to Satan's 'will' and did what he suggested in disobeying God, that omnipotence diminished to a limited authority. ***However***, (thank God for His 'however'), God brings authority back to us by means of a full salvation. Jesus, both before and after His resurrection, declares and speaks many things to mankind again to change situations and take away their vulnerabilities to Satan. He clearly says in the gospel, "These signs shall follow those that believe… In my name they shall cast out demons!" There's the power over Satan being manifest, right there. "They shall take up serpents!" There's the dominion over the rest of creation and in particular

A New Mission

the serpent that Satan used to deceive Eve. "If they drink any deadly thing it shall not harm them", there's our personal dominion over the elements! "They shall lay hands on the sick and the sick will recover", there's our dominion over things that dominate the body into submission".

This power over all things was declared to the disciples, such that wherever they went, they were never vulnerable. If they 'believed, all things were possible to them'. What would be the point, I ask, of God sending them out as ambassadors of His into the 'all the world' and them finding out that they could be 'shot down' as it were at the whims of evil? So God, when He sends his people out, arms them with abilities that He endues them with. Again, in the Acts 1 Jesus says, "You shall receive ***power*** (there's that word again) after the Holy Spirit is come upon you and you shall be witnesses to me!" Note too that when Jesus sends out the 70, they came back declaring that demons were subject to them. Jesus said, "I have given you power to trample upon snakes and scorpions" (there's that dominion again)… Heal the sick there!" Note also that this Dominion covered

A New Mission

'ALL the world' because Jesus said, "Go into ALL the world".

There's a lot for us to consider about our dominion because when we go as ambassadors of God 'Into all the world', we shouldn't be vulnerable as we go. I had a broken foot on one of my missions but God immediately healed it and got some glory for Himself out of the situation and I didn't even feel put out by it at all. I met with a Cobra on the banks of the Nile in Karuma, Uganda. I've never seen a live snake when I've been there but as the guide took us down to the river, to see the spectacular falls, it suddenly came to my mind that I had never seen any snakes, even though I had heard a lot about them. I asked the guide about it and he said, "Yes there are snakes here!" And 10 seconds later, he was stopping us in our tracks, "Look, there!", he said pointing in the tree just above our heads. In the tree that we were just about to walk under was a Cobra, ready to strike.

I don't know why I should have suddenly thought about snakes, ten steps before we got to the Cobra, except that while we're on God's mission, we're covered under the Mission covering of God.

A New Mission

While I was in Bible College, our Principal, Pastor Omri Bowen told us, "We were missionaries in Nigeria and one day we were invited to the local village chief's house. "We accepted", said the Pastor, "it was a great honour". We were served food and I gave thanks to God before we ate. As we began eating, the chief looked nervous and as we kept eating, he got very tense. After a while longer he looked extremely agitated and I had to ask him, what on earth was the matter?

The Chief suddenly blurted out, "I don't understand it!", watching the Pastor and his wife closely, "We put enough poison in the food to kill an elephant, and you don't die!" The Pastor explained to us, "It was part of our commission to go everywhere God sent us". He protected them everywhere. For me, 'Dominion' is not only something I believe in, it's something I preach too.

God's 'mission box' is full of everything we need. I remember Pastor Michael saying to me one year, "You know you should have a day off and rest a bit". He convinced me after a few years that maybe he was right and from there on we tried to get a day's rest on each mission. We would see

A New Mission

some of the game reserves or the source of the Nile or the beautiful Sipi Falls perhaps. One year we travelled to Murchison Falls game reserve in the west as I was in the area preaching at a convention in Loro. We had a great day, we saw Elephant and Zebra, Wart Hog, Giraffe, Hippos, Hyena, Monkeys and incredible waterfalls 200 feet high. As we left the reserve we headed down through the forest and eventually came out onto the main road. As we left the dust track, it was beginning to get dark and our driver, Jeff muttered something about the vehicle making a noise. We hadn't gone a few more metres before we had to pull up. They climbed underneath the engine and came out looking despondent but none the wiser.

We pulled across the road a few more metres on, next to a bus stop. As we looked at it again on more level ground where there was a little light from a nearby shop, a man came over. "What is the problem?" he asked. He was a mechanic and we had stopped right outside his premises, which was difficult to see in the dark. He reversed the vehicle a few metres down the bank into his workshop and said, "The half shaft bearings are gone but don't worry, I'll disconnect them, the 4

A New Mission

wheel drive will get you to Kampala, I'll tell you a guy who can do it there, I used to work with him, He's very good!"

He was right and ***what's more, right on time***. God ALWAYS took care of everything while we were on Mission and His timing is perfect. If Jesus had said it directly to me like He did to the disciples, it would have been no better than what we got while on mission. He is impartial to who does the preaching, as long as they have faith and you don't need clothes or anything while you're doing God's things, he will provide for you.

The resurrection is behind all of God's work in our lives and other people's lives. He brings LIFE to everything he touches. That's not only what He does, it's WHO He is. I try to remember that in all I do. If you need a situation fixed, He's the resurrector!

A mission is all about imparting newness of life to difficult or 'dead' situations, cultures, emotions, economies, etc.

A New Mission

Of course the FULL purpose of a mission is never seen. What goes on in the heart and soul of people touched by a mission is infinite because God's word goes on and on. Who knows what we unlock or lock up forever when God speaks through us?

A right person, in the right place where God wants them is priceless. I always remember hearing that when Billy Graham walked into a tent mission in the USA, he had never been to an evangelistic service before. He walked in and had a look around and was about to walk out again when an usher happened to see him. "Are you looking for a seat sir?" He asked. "Yes", came the reply, at which point the steward carefully selected a seat for him and showed him to it, doing a great job of ushering. In that service Billy Graham came to know Jesus as Saviour and Lord and the souls of millions getting born again, ensued. What is 'just a simple service' to many, in God's hands becomes mighty. You could say that the usher was 'on a mission' to just fulfil his function that day but he made a vital difference, as does everyone who fulfils their mission that God gives them to do.

A New Mission

Who knows WHO will come into the Kingdom of God when we go out on God's business? Who knows what difference that will make to the world?

A New Mission

CHAPTER ELEVEN

WHAT DO YOU PREACH?

When I first went to Uganda, the message God gave me was, "Tell my people they are forgiven!" I learned a great lesson that year in following what God said to do. Coupled with what He told me about not going ahead without Him and not to lag behind Him but to move WITH Him, I have learned some direct lessons but also some less direct lessons. As I've thought about those things that He said, I've learned patience but I've also found that, loyalty to God and WHO He is most important. We can drift into other things like the 'glamour'? or 'romance'? or conversely, going to a foreign country and doing 'charitable things'. I well remember visiting a village where we had provided hoes for digging and was told, "This is such a good thing, the villagers are calling them, 'Terry's Hoes'. I laughed initially but then thought to myself, 'No, They're not from me, they're from God and was quick to correct them. The whole point of the mission is to show God's

A New Mission

goodness and His mercy and His forgiveness. I wasn't about to turn the mission into 'Terry's mission.'

Preaching life is the right way for me, to revive people and places. I love preaching Faith. If you can lift people's faith, you can change people's understanding that they're not in a dead end, unable to get out, they're actually ABLE to lose that sinking feeling they are in because there's a God available who can do ANYTHING and help you at ANYTIME. I'll have returned home in a week or two or in a day or an hour or two but GOD is right there with them all the time, the next time they get a problem and He's a God who can do ALL THINGS. So it's not MY mission, it's GOD'S mission into their lives. So I left a message in the village with the church there. THESE ARE GOD'S HOES! HE helped you! The message is God's message, that what HE says will change your life, will inspire you, will raise you up. It's what HE does.

That vision of who God is, will get the backing of the Holy Spirit. He will endorse all you say when you declare that THIS GOD is a good God, that

A New Mission

He's there to help us, not to judge us. You may be surprised that putting right God's bad press that people so wrongly paint Him with, is a great message. It does YOU good too, to declare the right things about Him. I love correcting the lies about God and giving Satan and his supporters a blow that will set them back.

May I say that it also makes you bold to align yourself with truths and declare them because the alignment makes you strong, not only in your thinking but also in your personal confidence as you declare truth. Someone said, "The best doctrine is where you find out what God believes and agree with that". So 'want to know what to preach? Ask the Holy Spirit. **God is a maker, not a breaker**. The scriptures clearly say that, "A bruised reed, he will not break, a smoking flax He will not snuff out". If you are on your last legs, God will NOT finish you off, in fact He will support you and aid you the moment you give your life and situation over to Him and heal your brokenness.

While preaching in Loro in the north of Uganda at a convention, I had an interpreter, Justine Opuka

A New Mission

working with me. He told me his personal story one day about how he was fighting against the South Sudanese rebels with the Ugandan Militia. He said, "We were surrounded by the enemy, all my company had been killed except one and I was wounded, so I tried to protect him so that he could escape to safety. The rebels came into a clearing in the trees where I was and as I was wounded in the knee as a result of a bomb blast, I could not get away. As I lay there God spoke to me and said, 'Give your life to me'. I immediately handed over my life to God and as I did, a huge angel came and stood over me. As I lay there between his legs one of the rebels came and put a gun in my back and I waited for the shot. As he did so, his commander came into the clearing and said to him, "Don't waste a bullet on him, let's go!" They left and I got away. The man I had protected who escaped, got born again and became a Pastor and so did I".

Justine was a great interpreter for me on a number of occasions and a great evangelist. God's purposes in our lives are powerful. The message is that He is here to make your life better, stronger, healthier. If you are on a mission, tell people

A New Mission

about Him. Tell them WHO He is and WHAT He is, it will change their lives.

The message you preach is SO important. God is bigger than you think. Research who He is and preach that, not what you have heard about Him that is negative. The religious put a bad face on their interpretation of who and what God is. And when you preach who He is, you find out that YOU are bigger than you think, because you are made in His Image and Likeness and His presence is in you. His faith extends into you as you preach the truth and you find that you can do more than you could before because 'if you believe, all things are possible'.

I was preaching one year about WHO we are, that we are made in the image and likeness of God and filled with His Spirit. I had preached it around Uganda as we toured the towns and villages. As they heard it, many in congregations got healed at the realisation of this vision. Many came away with a new understanding that what God had made in the beginning in Adam and Eve's lives, God was *recreating* after salvation and bringing back full life to His people. Without touching them or

A New Mission

laying hands on people, they just got healed and set free. After touring Uganda that year, we then went over the border into Kenya on a mission, it becoming the first time I had ministered there. As we went over the border, I came to the Customs Control in Kenya.

The border control officer looked at me and said, "Papers please". I gave him the card I had filled in, detailing what I was going to do in Kenya, which read, "Missions Pastor, preaching etc". He took it, read it and gave a little smile. So I thought maybe we could have some humour, these situations are often tense and need a little fun added to them. As I gave him my passport, he looked at my photo on it and then looked at me matching the two up. I picked my moment and said to him in jest, "I apologise for the photograph, we have to have what nature hands out to us!" He went very serious and looked me straight in the face and said, "No sir, you are made in the image and likeness of God!" I was dumfounded. Here was I having come around 5,000 miles from the UK, talking to a complete stranger and God was telling me through him the message I had been preaching to everyone for 2 weeks in Uganda, a message that had

A New Mission

changed lives. God has some AMAZING ways for putting His point across and He doesn't leave the preacher out of the ministry either. He wants us ALL to know WHO WE ARE because it is SO important. When I got home, I lay in bed one morning and thought about the mission. My wife was still in the USA, visiting my daughter and I had the house to myself. As I lay there the remark at the Kenyan border came back to me and it just broke me, I sobbed and sobbed at the realisation that God wanted ME to know too how important I was to Him! <u>And that's the message</u>, that with God your life can be SO different. When you hand over all things to Him, He takes charge of your difficulties and weaknesses. "God is able to do exceedingly abundantly above all that you can ask and even think". I didn't make that up, God said it!

The message is also your testimony, your story of what God did for you. I believe that the most powerful thing you can tell is what God did in your life. WHY is that and why do I believe it? I believe that when God works in our lives, His word is established in us and people again behold His glory and once again, they will be amazed.

A New Mission

That thing He did, that salvation that changed your life, that miracle He did that healed you, that time He gave you peace, the moment He saved you from danger, they are all things you need to tell because people are literally dying, waiting, to hear what He can do because it means He can do it for them in *their* trial, in their trouble. The scripture says, "God is our refuge and our strength a VERY PRESENT help in the time of trouble!" These are the messages, there's not one message, there are so many and God wants to list the things that you can expect if you embark on a mission.

I was in Uganda recently and had been bitten wholesale by mosquitoes and my arms and ankles where I was exposed to the air, were itching and lumpy from their advances. There were also bites on my neck and even a bite on the top of my head where there was little blood for them to suck. In one place, I was happily preaching about who we are, made in God's Image and likeness and filled with His presence and that we were made to be like Him in all things and to have dominion again. I elucidated that we should, after redemption, start expecting to overcome things, preaching the dominion that faith should bring back to us. At

A New Mission

one point I said, rather off the cuff as it were, with faith rising in my message, "You know I'm just waiting for the day when African Christians stand up in their faith and say, "No more mosquito bites!" There was a hush for a moment and the whole congregation went silent as the words hit home and then the church erupted with euphoria and excited cheering. It added greatly to the message and I felt great about seeing so many grasp the point I had made. To my amazement the next day, as I put on my shirt, I looked at my arms and there were no bites. I mean, all the bites that were there, were **gone** and after that, listen to this, I had NOT ONE bite AT ALL for the remaining 10 days of the mission. Coincidence? No way! I just love the way God makes His point when He firstly gives us the word of faith, then does that 'crazy' extra thing to push the point home so that we finally 'get it'!

I remember hearing the story (and I'm relaying these stories to you so that you know that it's not just me) of how a missionary group went down into South America to the Amazon basin to reach tribes that had never heard the gospel. Day after day they waded through swamps and when they

A New Mission

returned to camp had to strip off and take a knife to scrape off the leeches that had attached themselves to them during the day. After a while one of the men said, with disdain and annoyance in his voice, "I'm fed up with these leeches. From now on NO MORE LEECHES, in Jesus name!" When they returned to camp the next day, they stripped off again but for this man, there were NO leeches and neither were there again, after that.

The scripture is full of examples where God gave dominion in so many places. Daniel defied the hierarchy of his land and refused to bow down to their god but instead opened his windows wide and prayed to HIS God in full view of all. He was duly put in the lion's den for his stand and God gave him dominion over the lions. It's amazing the way God takes the king of the jungle and suppresses him as an example for the sake of making His point.

During the plagues in Egypt the Israelites suffered nothing of what the Egyptians did. Locusts, frogs, lice, flies, boils, hail, murrain, darkness and the death of the firstborn etc. All passed them by. Jonah (yes I'm rubbing it in a bit) had the largest

A New Mission

sea animal act as a taxi to take him to shore when God gives him dominion over the whale.

Sometimes God goes to extraordinary lengths to show us who we are and that we can have dominion if we want it or need it. Some missionaries have gone into areas to take the gospel and despite the disease all around them, remained completely free from sickness. Dominion is a little talked about thing, it's almost like there's been a block placed on discussing it by the world and the church, that we're too civilised now and too 'scientifically wise' to consider these things but the fact remains, God gave Adam and Eve complete dominion over EVERY living creature. God hasn't changed His mind about who we are. We remain still His creation and He went to SUCH lengths to redeem us from the effects of the fall.

I don't think about the 'whys' and 'wherefores' of where I'm going and what I'm doing as I go on mission, that's not MY business, it's my business to speak the word of God and enlighten the people's minds about who they are. I'm not insensitive to my surroundings but when I have to

A New Mission

have my mind on other things, like the word of God, I need to give full attention to it and I expect God to take care of the rest. It's God's business to fulfil His side of the contract, to keep me from harm. I've been in churches on a few occasions where we have had armed police on the door but I deliberately don't consider the problems. I remember hearing Pastor Danny Nalliah from Pakistan telling of when he was in Saudi Arabia preaching and smuggling Bibles into the country. He said one day there were around 400 bibles on the table in the house and at that time, a loud knock came at the door. He went to the door and looked through the spyglass. Outside there were around 20+ men with automatic weapons.

He cried out as fear gripped him, "Jesus where are you?" He went into the back room and hugged his wife and children and returned to the door. As he did, God spoke to him and said, "My sheep hear my voice and NONE shall pluck them out of my hand". He opened the door and the leader of the men stared at him but said nothing. They stood looking at each other for a long time and he turned to his men occasionally, just looking at them but no one said anything. After a long while the man

A New Mission

spoke, "Papers!" Pastor Danny said, "I gave him my papers but he just stood there, saying nothing. Then God spoke to me again and said, 'I have allowed confusion to enter their minds so they don't know why they are here'. The man's silence went on for a while until finally he turned to his men and said, "Let's go", and they left." Pastor Danny said, "I wanted to shout 'hallelujah' but I remained quiet".

I'm sure God sent me those stories as I went out to Uganda, around the time that I started going there. It's important what we believe and God gave me many examples of people overcoming fear and just relaxing in God. It's important that we have peace in our hearts and minds. I keep saying to people, **"Our new creation doesn't know fear, it's unaware of what fear is, it's born of God and God is NOT afraid. *You can't scare Him.*** We tried our best when we flogged Him and when He hung on the cross but He went through with it, determined to redeem us from everything, fear included". If God isn't scared of it, then I'm doing my best with His help, not to be either, and I'm now seeing that it's my right to be free from fear.

A New Mission

You may consider that only missionaries get these privileges but that's another deception that Satan wants to spread. You are every bit as important to God. If you use your faith in everyday life, the miraculous will happen, "No plague will come nigh thy dwelling...., there shall no evil befall you! .... He will give His angels charge over you to keep you in all your ways". You don't have to go on mission to prove that. God just wants faith from you, exercised in everyday life for you to prove to yourself who you are and what God will do to make Himself and His ways known to you. You know if you think about it, life is one long mission. We set out to live and overcome all sorts of difficulties throughout it. We can do so with or without God, we can struggle with Satan and all his attempts to stop us or we can live our lives WITH God and see victory every day.

We don't have to go on mission to find out that we are covered by Him in all eventualities. Search the scriptures and see for yourself. As soon as you start looking, using your faith to find them, they appear so clear and so profoundly. They were there all along of course but our thinking, being brought up in sin and shaped by iniquity, filtered

A New Mission

them out. God gave you free will to decide if you want to overcome your problems, then He backs you up when you say, "Yes I want to do that"...... "I want an overcoming life!"..... "I want a life of Dominion!"

I cannot believe that God has any pleasure in seeing me run from Satan. It's that notion that makes me stand my ground, that as I see another onslaught arrive I think that God has made a way for me to overcome and as I preach, other people need the faith to make a stand too. I am aware that as others have fed my faith with the word of God and gave me courage to believe, so I need to pass on that courage to others. As I was talking one day to one group of ladies who were about to go into the town to 'encourage' people, I realised that what was really required was that they GAVE people courage, which was actually what they were saying but the trouble is we lose the meanings of words sometimes.   Preaching the right things will give people courage to believe for what God has promised that we can have. Preaching with understanding of what we are doing will sharpen our words into a faith filled message that inspires.

A New Mission

A New Mission

CHAPTER TWELVE

RADIO MINISTRY AND OTHER THINGS

Mission in Africa led me to new ventures. While in the north I was privileged, while up in Kitgum to speak on Radio. 'Mighty Fire FM' (a great name isn't it?) is run by faith and covers over a million people. As I preached on air, I was aware that I was totally comfortable with it. If you had asked me some years before to go on the air and speak on radio, I would have been nervous maybe, I would have had to be totally prepared and 'tuned up' ready to do it. The fact was, however, totally different to that, I was relaxed, excited, enthusiastic and at home with doing it. Now that amazes me as I look back at it and even at the time it did too. Even as we were on air, it struck me that I was doing this OK and wasn't nervous or anything. Strange! So did God always do things this way? I mean, does He always enable us so easily? I would say no but since losing fear and

A New Mission

doing more things, I did start to do things in my stride as it were, which shocked me really.

This wasn't me. At one time, before preaching I would pace my bedroom or my study needing to know the message well, be rehearsed and everything had to go just right. That was fear doing that, I was worried about my inability, concerned that I didn't know the message. Would I get the right response from the congregation? All the negatives would play out. When the time came, however, God had already done a work in me. He knew that of course and there's the pillar of fire thing again, "Don't go without me, stick with me!" I did and everything was fine.

As I ministered on air I realised that my times as a sound engineer and a preacher and running summer fetes in villages at home all came together in one and I saw that God had already trained me for this. As we prayed for the sick on air after preaching, we had callers phoning in their requests for prayer. I remember a young man called Samuel saying "I have pains in my stomach, please will you pray for me?" The following morning as we were on air again, he rang in again. "As you

A New Mission

prayed last evening, all my pains went!" That was another aspect of ministry I needed to hear positive results from. In my mind, it was one thing to go on air and pray for the sick, it was another thing to see the right results. Sometimes we need to be just thrown into it and have to get on with it, without preconceived ideas and just trust God, and see things just happen, because God has it covered.

We left money there to support the radio station and for the orphanage attached to the church. The people of Victory Church UK had given me some funds before I left and it was a privilege to go and meet needs with it. God bless those who have been so faithful in providing the means to bless His people abroad. Several other Radio stations, 'Rukungiri Radio' in the South and 'Mercy FM' in Mbarara and Rock Mambo FM in Tororo are also places we went to preach the word of God on air as well as local 'radio' in Kyanga, Uganda, which was more of a wired network around town with loudspeakers that fed certain areas.

Missions involve you going to many areas that you may not normally consider. Prison ministry was not one that I was prepared for as I thought but

A New Mission

God had other ideas. Once again, I found He had already 'prepped' me for the moment. We went into Soroti prison in middle Uganda one year and I spoke to 583 prisoners. I was surprised as so many gathered in the prison yard were interested in what we had to say. There was a group in the prison of Born Again inmates who had started a Christian Union sort of ministry. I was invited to go in and share what I had. I often share my testimony of how I became a believer, how God healed me of Asthma and any other thing that God puts on my mind. I AM ALWAYS AMAZED at what comes out of those sessions. As I told them my story that day, I noticed many hanging on my every word. We prayed and committed everything to God, many gave their lives to Him and we left happy in the knowledge that this time had been profitable.

When I spoke that day I told them how that God had given me sleep as an Asthmatic and relayed the scripture to them that He gave me which brought about my miracle, Proverbs 3:24, "When you lie down, you will not be afraid, You will lie down and your sleep will be sweet." As we got out of the prison yard, one of the wardens, who was a Christian, said to me, "Of course, you realise

A New Mission

that many prisoners cannot sleep!" I said "Really?" "Yes", he said, "they are worried about their families, they are the breadwinner in their family and they are concerned about their wives and children starving". I was just completely taken aback at how God had used the word that day. Another example of how He is Lord over every situation when you undertake to live with Him in your life.

In Kitgum prison I was asked to speak to around 330 male prisoners and 55 female prisoners. Many, around 40 residents got saved that day and my testimony, my life story went well again. You know, that's what gets to people hearts, what God did in **your** life. They seem to love hearing the story of what Jesus really did in a real life. We realised too that prisoners have needs.

In many African prisons they get no privileges, just very basic needs. So we learned to take in things that make some difference for them. In this case it was boxes of soap for all the prisoners and sanitary items for the female prisoners to help maintain their dignity while in prison. They also had no shade from the sun as they met in the

A New Mission

prison yard for their Christian services so we bought them a huge tarpaulin that they could string up as a sun shade. 'Only a small thing to do but it has a big bearing on how they perceive our visit and the shade attracts other prisoners to the service.

In Masaka Prison, we were only allowed to speak to the Governor, preparing the way for visits in the future but as we talked, we were able to tell of the differences God had made in the lives of prisoners elsewhere. He was impressed that we took the time to even consider visiting prisoners. In Kyanga we visited the Police Headquarters where there were many Christian officers. We met the Chief of Police and sat in his office. When he finished a phone conversation, he put aside his papers and we explained that we would like to pray for him and his staff that God would give them protection and help them with their work. He was very thankful and was also impressed when we told him of our drug and alcohol rehabilitation unit back home and the miraculous things God is doing with our young men. I believe the future will see the local church there in Kyanga working

A New Mission

with the police to set up a similar system to tackle problems in their community.

The things God does in our lives can be shared to great effect and work with addicts is a great ministry. I'm stunned by the changes God makes in the lives of addicts. I'm so impressed that when God saves them and they come off their drugs and alcohol how nice these people are and what an awful shame it is that their lives were interrupted by bad habits but once again God can give people dominion again over these things. I was reading Galatians chapter 5 again recently, I love reading what the fruits of God's Spirit are, it shows what God's Spirit is capable of in our lives. One of those 'fruits' is temperance. God can 'restore self control to us', is what the scripture is really saying. In other words, God puts you back in charge of your life whereas before anyone or anything was in charge of it. God's free will is transferable to you, therefore He gives you your free will back, the ability to decide your own future.

Galatians 5 also says, "Brethren you have been called to liberty!" Thank God for his ennablement

A New Mission

in our lives, it makes us free and that's as much of the message we preach as anything else.

A New Mission

CHAPTER THIRTEEN

PRODUCTS OF PREACHING

I am always amazed when I get a report of what has happened in places when I preach. I think it's because seeing faith work, which is an invisible power and to see it working when I speak things that God says, is more amazing because now ***I'm*** involved in the process. There's also that lingering self-doubt that we have got used to throughout our lives that God is slowly dispersing as He gives us more faith and the confidence that comes with it. I wonder sometimes, if faith continues to grow in us and becomes a natural thing to us, which I believe ***should*** happen, will there be ANY doubt left in any of our being then? There has to be a related effect whenever God's gifts grow in us.

One day when I was speaking in a big church in Masaka, south east of Uganda alongside lake Victoria, I was again speaking about who we are and what God made us to be in the beginning. They had been fasting and praying and I spoke in

A New Mission

the lunch hour to a fairly large number in the congregation. At the end of every message I always call people to a commitment of some description, dependent on where the Lord leads me in the message. This day was no different. The next day a lady came up to me after I had spoken in their 'Morning Glory' breakfast service. She said, "Pastor, I have to tell you, I have been suffering with back pain for a long time now but as you spoke yesterday, all my pain disappeared!"

I may be slow sometimes to lay hands on the sick, being taken up often with the message but when speaking God's word does the work alone, it always gives me a buzz. I think of that time when the Roman centurion comes to Jesus and says, "Just speak the word only and my servant will be healed!" It's great when people just believe what God says and then see things happen but miracles happen in different ways. When I was in Tororo in the East one afternoon speaking to a small church congregation of around 30-40 people, I was drawn to the subject of the Fruits of the Holy Spirit in Galatians 5 again. As I spoke of the power of God and His ways, I made the statement, "You know when God made Adam, He breathed into him the

A New Mission

breath of life and gave him all of Himself, but on the day of Pentecost there came a sound from Heaven like a mighty rushing wind. I believe God was breathing into His people again to bring them life."

As I said it, I was aware that God was telling us to be proactive about it and as God breathed on them, then we should breathe Him in. It rather followed what Jesus said when He breathed on people and told them to 'receive the Holy Spirit'. As people all over the church breathed in the Spirit of God, they began to shake and weep, many just breaking down as release came to them from their problems. I noticed a lady over on my right of the church. She just broke down completely and sobbed. I laid hands on many that day and many had release from their afflictions but this lady got healed of breast cancer that afternoon.

In Africa's often difficult situation with regard to health and poor health treatment availability, God is the only answer and the only one standing between them and death. In the south in Kabale recently I was asked to speak at a youth service. I told some of my life story again and we prayed for

A New Mission

many young people afterwards. A young man approached me and asked if I would pray for him. "Sure" I said. "What's the problem?" "I have epilepsy", he said. So I spoke to the epilepsy and told it to leave him and released peace to him and healing. We had a phone call a few days later from his mother to say that the epilepsy had gone. Also in that youth service I laid hands on a young man who had stomach pains and was worried about what it was. I spoke to fear in him and released peace to him and again we had a phone call a day later that all his pains had gone.

I think what comes across so often to me is that we go into differing situations and meet people with such varied problems but God is equal to them all. We can be reluctant to tackle things we've never seen before or been asked to pray for before but taking the opportunity will bring a result if we just believe for it, whatever it is. I'm never perturbed if it doesn't happen just then when we pray, it happens in God's time, the wheels are set in motion when we pray believing. I was reminded recently that people often don't appear healed but when we pray, often the 'blockage' to their healing is removed, paving the way for healing to now take

A New Mission

place. That type of prayer may be needed a few times perhaps but eventually healing will come. That was the criteria that Jesus gave when he spoke about faith, He said, If YOU believe, all things are possible. Faith is activated when we speak. Again Jesus said, "If you have faith you will SAY"….. What you 'say' depends on your situation. In the situation He was speaking of, He said, "You will SAY to this mountain, be removed and it will obey you". Whatever your mountain is, whatever is in your way, however big it is, if God says it will move if you use your faith, *it **will** move.*

Speaking God's faith to people is the most rewarding to preach. If you want to start a revolution in people's lives preach faith to their hearts. If you want to destroy Satan's power in this world, preach faith, get active, pray for the sick or pray life into situations. Give God the opportunity to move people's problems out of their lives, speak to the problems what God wants you to say that will encapsulate their need. Preaching is not all about bringing people to salvation in Christ Jesus, that is, getting them to make that first step of asking God into their lives. Many have

A New Mission

already done that but need to get over the problems that their bad-habit forming flesh ties them into on a daily basis. Showing people scripture that tells them how to overcome sin in their flesh and do away with the things that distract them from who they are, is a great pastime. You may not think of preaching as a pastime but to enjoy giving people things that changes their lives is enjoyable, it gives you joy. Seeing people stand up and be counted when they have been oppressed and suppressed and depressed by Satan is a great thing to see. It makes you realise who we are and what God made us and wants us to be.

The other thing about preaching is that you can impart revelation to people that makes them grow spiritually. Ultimately, and I know I have spoken much of it in this book, the full revelation of who we are will destroy all sickness, disease, fear, sin, weakness, torment, pain, demonic power, and ALL the problems of man. A great prayer to pray is, **"Father in Heaven, express all of yourself through all of me, fully"**, because in this we show all our desire for God-likeness but preaching can also inspire people to know completeness in God, or 'being perfect' as Jesus commanded us to be.

A New Mission

Missions therefore, whether small or big, far away from or near to home, declare faith that takes people places in their lives. *Improvement must always be the aim,* **God ALWAYS seeks to better us, to make us bigger, to improve our vision, make us healthier, give us more initiative, increase the life in us,** *decrease the death in us,* **give us more joy, increase our peace, make us more durable (longsuffering), help us love more, to make us good, to give us more faith, to put us in charge of every area of our lives again, to liberate us.** *There are more things that can be added to this list, maybe there are things in your life that you need that are not there.* **Well, just ask the Almighty for those things and believe for them.**

CHAPTER FOURTEEN

THE RISEN LORD

I keep saying it, that behind all our regeneration, rejuvenation, rebuilding and rehabilitation is the one great character that does it all, the character of the Almighty God. **We need to concentrate more on who God is.** He is clearly one who creates. He is clearly also, following that line through, a God who *recreates* and is therefore one who resurrects dead and old things. Remembering who spoke the worlds into being, we see one who from His mind and His thinking spoke out of His heart too when He created. **This is A New Mission God.** *It's what He is.* His whole being is forged together as one of making good things and creating life. As He rises from the dead a new dawn breaks in the life of mankind. This is where dominion really takes off for the whole world. Jesus' declaration that they should address the WHOLE WORLD with His gospel, is significant. "Go teach all nations, baptising them in the name of the Father, the Son and the Holy Spirit". This is a revolution

A New Mission

to affect the WHOLE <u>world because it's the whole world that He loves</u>, it's the whole world that He died for, it's the whole world He created in the beginning and made in His own image, in His own likeness and filled with His Own Spirit. We cannot divorce Genesis and who Adam and Eve were from who we are now. They were His full intention in their 'pre-fall state'. All that they were, we must become again because a *full* salvation was planned *for us all*.

It's significant that after His resurrection, Jesus continues the 'new world' process. Out of that single event, when the dead came to life, the worst event in a life was reversed by the power of God's Spirit. When all the physical life had gone from His body, when all His emotions were dead, when all His resolve and life was gone, when all His initiatives had stopped, when all His activity in every area was negated and still, out of that tomb came a fully living being again. The Holy Spirit reached into the tomb and began His resurrecting influence. The body began to repair. Every cell that had died revived and was recreated. It's fundamentally important that we get to grips with the full revelation of what happened that morning.

A New Mission

The heart that was starved of oxygen and died, was remade and lived again, the pancreas, the lungs, the brain, the muscles, the nerves, the bones, - all became new and life supporting again. The heart started pumping again, blood flowed again in the newly reconstituted veins and was taken to every part revitalising them and warming them.

The stomach worked and digested again, the lungs refreshed the body once more with oxygen, everything worked perfectly again as the Spirit of the living God pervaded every cell.

It's from this standpoint that all salvation-change in us is begun. Some people have failed to grasp this and been unable to connect their beliefs with the full notion of resurrection. "Perhaps He wasn't really dead, when they took Him down from the cross", some have even said. The fact that, with all His wounds which were fatal ones, He lay unattended medically for three days in a cold tomb and He couldn't have survived that, has gone totally unnoticed by some. There were some overwhelming and significant factors that meant He was fully dead. The soldiers that came to break the legs of those crucified that day, testified that

A New Mission

Jesus was already dead. Then a soldier pushed a spear into His side and it says, "there came out blood and water". There's only one place in the body where water can come from in those circumstances. From the angle at which the soldier stood when he put the spear in, which was from the ground to Jesus' elevated position, it would have entered under the ribs and into the heart region. As Jesus hung there, scientists say that His heart would have been working extremely hard to keep going under His dire circumstances. The pericardium around the heart would have become like a huge blister from the inflammation caused by it and the area around the heart would have filled with water. If the spear entered that area and the pericardium was punctured, death would have been immediate. They tell me that's the only place water could have come from.

Why am I stating these things? It's because if we don't come to terms with the idea that Jesus fully died, then we can't be saved because our 'resurrection in spirit, soul and body, depends on it. But He died, fully and completely and the Holy Spirit raised Him fully and completely and THAT is the principle on which a FULL salvation takes

A New Mission

place. ALL that was dead became alive again. Life was restored to one, the precedent was set legally and physically, actively and emotionally for ANYONE who needed resurrection after that, to receive it and ***fully receive it.*** I remember preaching those words about the Holy Spirit's work in the tomb, raising Jesus from the dead, in a service in Karuma Uganda, describing the events that went on in His body, making each part alive again. It had an amazing effect on the congregation, raising their faith and making many think again.

We had some great results that day, many rededicating their lives to the risen Lord. After the service the Pastors led me outside and asked me if I would come and pray for a lady who was 'very sick'. I asked them as we walked, "What's wrong with her?" "She has a very bad heart, she is very ill", they replied. We walked a few metres away from the church to a nearby grass-roofed house.

When we entered the house, they showed me the lady who lay on a mat on the floor in the rear area of the hut. The lady was covered completely with a sheet and lay motionless, at least, I saw no

A New Mission

movement at all and there was no response to anything I did. As I approached her, I crouched down, almost kneeling and laid my hands on her and started to pray. As I did so there was no response or movement whatsoever. I couldn't feel her breathing and she didn't stir at all when I prayed and I was not silent in prayer, in fact I was quite loudly vocal, not overly so but I didn't mince words, this lady was sick and I discharged what was in my heart about the matter. Happy that I had prayed what I felt I had to, releasing peace and life and healing to her, I stood up. There was still no response at all from the lady. She lay there completely still with the sheet fully covering her from head to toe.

The others had arrived at the door by now and I greeted them as they came in to the house. They were local Pastors and the Evangelist who translated for me that day when I spoke. I was a little distracted by their entrance and not wanting to ignore them in any way, met their entry with a handshake and a smile, with some of them being introduced to me. I turned around and looked in the lady's direction, speaking about what we had been doing for the past couple of minutes and as I

A New Mission

did so, the blanket slipped back and the lady sat up with a smile and looked at me and we shook hands. She looked fine and the room went quiet as we all looked at each other in amazement. It wasn't until later when I realised how sick she was that I recognised just what God had done there that day.

Mission is a great practice because it is a task force, an objective, an incursion to take what is dead and speak life to it, invading the dead area and pushing life into it's core. The labels given to God are that He is LIGHT and LIFE. Light drives out darkness, you notice that darkness is totally dominated by light as soon as it appears and we see the darkness disappear. Life also dominates death as we can see from the resurrection of Jesus. As a human race, we never considered that death was beatable until the Bible told us about it.

Mission, as I've said is not necessarily a visit abroad to preach the gospel, it can be the changing of a life anywhere, in an individual anywhere, anyone at all. We often limit God by our thinking but the Holy Spirit is capable of restoring power to any being FULLY at any time. The Holy Spirit

A New Mission

teaches us a NEW way that we hadn't formerly considered, that life is possible again where death currently reigns. The thing is, resurrection changes all the rules that we exist by, it opens up new vistas, raises many questions and challenges the status quo in ways that we didn't see coming. Resurrection places hope at the heart of us where there was or is no hope. It creates a new situation that we couldn't formerly see. It puts an exit, a way out into our vision where there was no escape route before. We SO need revelation from the Holy Spirit to enlighten our lives about what is available to us. If we have no idea of what *can* happen with faith, then we are losing out and that's sad because God has provided so much for us.

God spoke to us in a Sunday morning service in a Midlands Church though a prophet. He said, "When you are surrounded and you appear to be trapped with no way out, look for the way of escape, ***because I have provided one!***" Now that's a pretty broad statement for us to try and accept but I didn't say it, **God said it!** As soon as I heard it, my mind went into exuberant and joyous ecstasy. Here was a statement from God my soul was waiting for. I started going through the

A New Mission

scenarios in my mind, "Do you mean Lord that when I'm …… there's a way out?" The answer came back "YES" at every scenario I envisaged and as I examined scripture in the light of the possible predicaments that I could get into, God backed it up with examples of where He had saved His people before.

The Risen Lord is the key to all our overcoming. What happened when Jesus rose from the dead affects us all. **Rising from the dead** and overcoming the biggest enemy of man that has the most final effect on us, **destroys the threat completely if you align yourself with it.** Jesus, in rising from the dead rises above every threat to man. It's why scripture (Romans 10. 9) says, "If you confess with your mouth that Jesus is Lord and believe in your heart that God raised him from the dead, you will be saved. You see, we have to align ourselves with it for it to be so. So confess it, believe it, eat it and drink it, let the idea LIVE in you. Make it your founding principle in life such that nothing is allowed to dominate it. LIFE HAS to be the pre-eminent force in us, as it is in the Almighty, then our life works as it should.

A New Mission

It becomes victorious and stands where others fail. It remains where others diminish and run out. Any venture into a new area with God will change that new area. What it was before is going to alter because light has arrived, darkness must now disappear and everything unseen will now be seen.

Imagine entering a room full of darkness, you would very gingerly step forward feeling the floor ahead with your foot, investigating what's there. It could have any amount of traps set for you. You have no idea of the parameters of that room, it could have a high ceiling or a very low ceiling, a hole or several holes in the floor, obstacles to trip over, cables to electrocute you, any amount of things designed to destroy you. But as soon as light appears, you suddenly understand everything about the room, all the traps and snares are readily apparent. God's Spirit is a teacher. He sheds light on everything ahead of you. That same Spirit that Jesus speaks of in John 14:26 that, "Will Teach you all things" is the same one that raised Jesus from the dead and, says Romans 8:11, "...If He dwells in you, He will make you alive too. He's the 'resurrector'. That's my second use of this

A New Mission

word (apparently it's not known by the spell checker) but it's a good word. The Holy Spirit is the one you need to do the work of making you alive and teach you stuff that you need to know for all things that make you overcome. He will, 'Take of the things of Jesus and reveal them to us', to remind us of what Jesus said. He will also take of the activities that happened to Jesus when He was resurrected and make those things, those new ways, notions and principles known to you. Those things that Jesus spoke changed our world. He said in front of Lazarus's tomb, "I am the resurrection and the life!" A Mission will inevitably involve speaking Jesus' words if this world is to change.

A New Mission

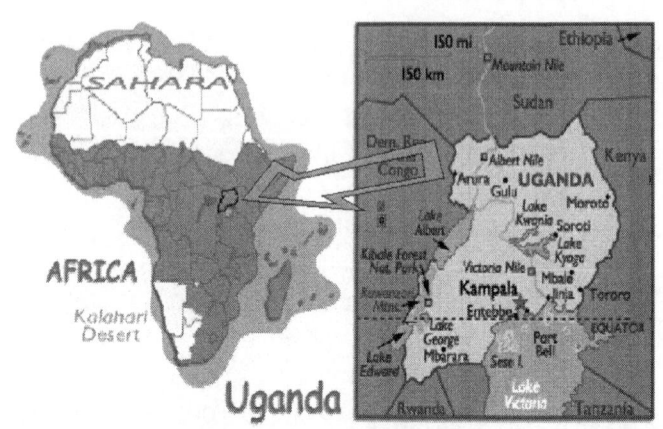

Where is Uganda? -Eastern Central Africa, located just above Lake Victoria.

The Kings Primary School, Bunambutye, Uganda.
14 Classes, 20 Staff, 435 pupils.

A New Mission

Some of our children at Kings Primary School

Pupils hard at work.

A New Mission

Local Villages houses where our children live

New Hoes for Villagers

A New Mission

In the Presidents Office

Right on the Equator

A New Mission

Hoes and seeds for Villagers

Mount Rwenzori

A New Mission

Mount Rwenzori Convention

Giving their lives to Jesus at Mount Rwenzori

A New Mission

Rabbits Bred by the Pastor, for food!

One of Uganda's Largest Christian Secondary Schools

A New Mission

A Growing Church in Mbale Town.

Pastors Meeting before the Convention in Loro

A New Mission

Salt Lakes

Guest Speaker at an African Wedding.

A New Mission

Baboons at the roadside

A Lion at Kasesi

A New Mission

Giraffe at Murchison Falls National Park

Zebra at the roadside in the North of Uganda

A New Mission

Lioness at Queen Elizabeth National Park

Uganda's Natural Beauty

CHAPTER FIFTEEN

THE MISSION OF THE HEART OF GOD

I've left this subject late in this book because it should be one of the foremost in our minds as we consider a mission of any kind and therefore one of the last things you might remember reading perhaps, about the book. The reason God took so much time over us and thought so much about saving us is that His heart dictated it to Him because we are **His** people, the ones **He** created and loved. The scripture says, "God is Love".

So much has been said about God though and people always hold up this phrase when defending their position not to trust or believe in God and love Him: "If God is love, then why doesn't He stop this happening or that happening?" Bad things happen when people use the free will that God gave them, to do evil things. But really, - God **is** LOVE! There's nothing contrary to that which He is. There's no change in God or

A New Mission

variance in Him, He is true and loyal, TRUTH in fact.

The whole motivation of God to save us and redeem us from the position we were in, is LOVE. When we speak of love, we often use the phrase, rightly, 'the heart of the Father'. As we are made in three parts, Body Soul and Spirit, so is God, we are made in His Image, His likeness and filled with His Spirit - His presence. The Father is the soul of the Trinity, The son is the physical part - God manifest in flesh and the Holy Spirit is the third part, the Life of God. The Father is the passion and decision maker, Jesus did nothing but that the Father told Him to do it or say it. God is LOVE, there's the passion side of Him. Of course, when we see God manifest in flesh, we see occasions when He weeps, He shows passion, He displays compassion, He speaks to people directly.

When Philip says, to Jesus, "Show us the Father and that will be enough for us!" God speaks directly to him out of Jesus's mouth, "Have I been so long with you and you haven't known me Philip?" I feel sometimes that we haven't unravelled the 'mystery' of the Trinity because

A New Mission

that's what it has become to so many and we lose out when we don't understand that He is what we are, made in three parts, exactly like Him. We have passions and compassion, we have love, we have a sense of justice, we love fair play, we see other people's needs, we 'feel sorry for them' (pity). So many of the attributes God has, we display, even in our sinful state.

But when we come to a mission of any kind, that mission must be the result of us obeying the call of God in our lives, a response to people's needs highlighted to us by the Spirit of God conveying the feelings and heart of the Almighty when He sees their needs. To me, that should be <u>the criteria for a mission.</u> We can do good things in a cold and calculated way but what captures the hearts of people, which God desires most, is when we feel for the people that we minister to and it becomes evident that love is foremost in our character, just like the Almighty's. God IS love.

What greater transmission of life can there be to someone than when someone gives good things with a heart that feels their need and reacts to it? We have a reaction from the whole person when

A New Mission

we see that happen. The heart of the person feels the hurt and need of an individual, it goes into the mind and then they make a decision to help, which is then acted upon and they physically give to the need of that individual. And I think right there we have it, Jesus said, "Therefore everyone who hears these words of Mine and acts on them is like a wise man who built his house on the rock." What God wants from us is for us to hear the good teachings of Jesus and then for us to act on them, to hear the story of the good Samaritan and react to it, to feel the needs of people and do something for them. When our whole being, spirit, soul and body gets involved with goodness, ***then*** God gets the glory.

I've called this chapter, "The mission of the heart of God". I want to create the understanding that God wants to affect the lives of His people, to repair those lives, to bring peace to them, to show love to them, to release joy in them, to make them endure and to make them good again in all things. We have somehow shelved the idea of becoming totally good, I've heard so many glibly say, "Well we'll never be perfect, only God is perfect" and in that instance, out of the door goes any

A New Mission

understanding of what work God can do in us. In that moment we lose the feeling of a possibility of us becoming good and perfect as Jesus commanded us to be. I often look at that verse where Jesus says, "Be perfect therefore as your Father in Heaven is perfect" (Matthew 5:48) and wonder what we have done with it. Also in 1 Peter 1. 15,16 "But just as he who called you is holy, so be holy in all you do; for it is written: 'Be holy, because I am holy.'"

When we go on a mission we need our faith unbridled and unfettered, we need ourselves released to be what God made us in the beginning to be, whether we are faced with impossible odds in the jungle or faced with a bad flu cold at home, faith has the ability to do what we need. We forget that in the beginning God gave Adam and Eve all that He had, He gave Himself fully into their beings. THEN he spoke words over their lives, ETERNAL WORDS of *enablement*. He said "BE fruitful, multiply, replenish!" Those words were spoken over us all in Adam and Eve. All coming after them would feel the power of those commands. We may have negated much of the effect of those words but they are ETERNAL

A New Mission

words. Nothing that God speaks can be rubbed out, it's there for ever for us to take up. We can negate the effect of what He said but not the intention and the commission of what He said. Those words are still here in the earth, "BE FRUITFUL", ('Have good results from what you do!") "MULTIPLY", ('All that you do will get bigger!') "REPLENISH", ('Put back what has been diminished!'). God is not putting on us a responsibility to try and be something that we cannot, He is speaking an enabling word to us that brings us to *where* He wants us to be and *what* He wants us to be. We seem to forget that when God speaks, His will is revealed and all of those commands for things to BE what he intends, are still awaiting completion. We complete them when we use our faith to put them into being.

A mission that He sends us on, is like His words, it has in it the core of what He feels in His heart for the ones He is sending us to meet. I've spoken of His 'Missions Box' that contains all the kit we need for the mission but I didn't say that to release those things, you need God's heart to let them go to the needy. Naturally, being born in sin and shaped in iniquity, when we get possessions, we

A New Mission

hold onto them, it's part of the poverty trap we have lived in. We are often reluctant to let go of things because we have lived poorly and we don't want to get poorer so we live in that frugal realm. To let them go we need a bountiful heart, the same as the Father's to release the bounty He has endued us with. There's everything in us, by faith, that the world needs.

Our Father in Heaven put it there. He also gave us the heart to release it, He gave us His love. When Jesus taught us to pray, the first thing He told us to do, was to "SAY". He does away with the 'prayer' thing and goes the direct route and says, "SAY".... Then He tells us WHAT to 'say'. Firstly He says, SAY, "OUR FATHER, WHO IS IN HEAVEN". I.E, when you enter the world of problems to change those situations, SAY who you are! "My Father who is in Heaven!" Now all that are listening, whether in the physical world or in the Spiritual world around us, are aware of who we are. We need an awareness of our identity especially when we are on a mission, so say who you are. As we step into situations, we need to declare who we are and WE need to remember it

A New Mission

too. We are Children of the living God. The phrase, "My Father", says it clearly.

We have His heart too, we forget that we are new creations now that we are born again. We are born once more but this time with a birth that is without the weaknesses of sin. Our flesh may still have bad habits that show us to be things that we are not but our 'innermost man' is a different creature. We have a heart now. We used to have a heart of stone but now we have a heart of flesh, one that beats and feels emotions. The heart of the Father is just like that and goes and seeks out those in need. <u>A mission must be the same</u>. It should seek out what people need and provide it. That may be to give revelation of who they are, to pull them out of their misconceptions of who they are so that they can start living as overcoming believers. It may be to give them faith for *what* they need, salvation, healing, deliverance, prosperity, life......

The heart of God is a feeling heart. When I say that, God is always looking at our needs and hearing the cries of our hearts. Often we don't have to say a word but He sees what we really need, which may be hidden to even ourselves.

A New Mission

When we preach or minister, it's so important to listen to the Holy Spirit to hear what we should say to congregations, don't forget that we are there to speak right into their hearts what they have been waiting to hear. You know, whether we realise it or whether the people themselves realise it, there are things we are all crying out for. Cries from deep within sometimes go on for years. People sink them to the bottom of their being and hide their emotions, subjugating them and relegating them to become things of less importance because they don't have a hope of ever having those things sorted out. Sickness, fears, disease, weaknesses, poverty, loneliness, love, friendship, comfort, are all things people need tending to. They often don't even know what they need, let alone that they can ask God for their requirements.

A mission can encapsulate all their hidden cries, if the preacher is tuned in to the 'listening heart' of God. If you think that's an odd phrase, **well, we can learn to listen with our hearts.** We can learn to 'see' people's needs. I'm not talking about the obvious, visual things but with wisdom, discernment and understanding we can see the spiritual matters that the world doesn't see and the

A New Mission

hidden things that are destroying lives and families. Taking the leading of the Holy Spirit along to minister with, is vital.

I always remember a young woman coming, sobbing, after I preached and asking for help because she couldn't hug her son. She said, "I want to and I know he is looking for me to love him but I just can't bring myself to do it!" A word of knowledge came and the Holy Spirit revealed that there was incest in the family background. At first she angrily called it 'nonsense'. Then after a while as it was revealed to her, she spoke of how it came about in her family and how it affected her. I told her, "The problem works like this, you want to do what is right because you want righteousness, so you're afraid that if you hug your son, you're afraid you would contaminate him with the curse that is on the family so you push him away to protect him". She breathed a sigh of relief and asked what could be done. We spoke to the family curse telling it to leave and released her so she could love her son properly.

The problem is that many lives are 'tied up' and some have few emotions because of hidden problems that only God sees. The heart of God feels for us when our hearts cry out. A mission needs us to use 'all the best gifts' of the Holy Spirit and we should covet them in order to be good 'missionaries'.

A New Mission

CHAPTER SIXTEEN

"JERUSALEM, JUDEA, SAMARIA AND TO THE UTTERMOST PARTS OF THE EARTH....."

"Go into all the earth and preach the gospel to every creature". That's the mandate from Jesus. The call often starts off small, even in a whisper from God as it were but the amazing thing is that a mission often takes the holds off **us**. Anything the Almighty has you doing, will increase you.

A mission is a great venture for releasing our faith and making us grow. Not only the mission areas in the world grow but we get to grow too. And.... Jesus said, "You shall receive power after the Holy Spirit is come upon you and you shall be witnesses of me... In Jerusalem and in Judea and in Samaria and to the ends of the earth". There's a great progression here in this scripture. It begins with the Holy Spirit and what happens when He comes to us, when we invite Him into our lives and what the effect of that is. Literally, the word 'Dunamis'

A New Mission

used here in the greek text of Acts 1:8 is translated as the word 'power' in English.

Many preachers have used the comment, "This is the same word we get 'dynamite' from." I don't see the connection, I think it's a flamboyant statement that doesn't, for me, fit the case. Dynamite is destructive. The Holy Spirit's work is to teach (he's a counsellor). His work is also to resurrect (to raise from the dead) and to comfort (He is the comforter) and liberate us. I see no overwhelming blast like dynamite from God here, only consensual teaching of all the things that make us live and be comforted and make us liberated. OK, it's nice to think that when we utilise God's Spirit to release us from Satan's grip, that a sudden, strong, power breaks our chains and releases us but in reality the Holy Spirit teaches us who we are, that we have AUTHORITY over Satan. Now that may come as a hammer blow to Satan but for us, it's a progressive and gentle realisation that NOTHING has power over us. The Holy Spirit is LIFE, not death. He enlivens the dead parts of us and 'Quickens' (the older English word used in scripture) us.

A New Mission

In this scripture we see a progression in terms of land being evangelised, Jerusalem, Judea, Samaria.... the world but what is happening in a mission sense, is that as we go and do the mission and 'we grow as we go'. I think of Joshua and what God told him, "As I was with Moses, so shall I be with you, I will not fail you or forsake you... Every place that the sole of your foot shall tread on I have given you!"

Now that is a progression. Footstep after footstep, claiming new territory. Every place is different, every place is a different challenge and poses differing personal tests. To overcome them and progress makes you more confident at every turn, and in terms of the promise to Joshua, it's in every stride, in every footstep! Many can't cope with new challenges but Jesus I think gives a great piece of advice to us. He said, "When you go to a place and they don't accept you.... Shake the dust off your feet and move on". For me that means, don't take the rejection of the last place with you, leave the memory of it behind and start a new day with active new faith and new confidence. There's an overcoming power in that, it means you don't let the losses faze you but you forget the negativity

A New Mission

of the event and pass over it. God is in every day and in every footstep you take and puts victory into those steps. Moving on from a difficulty is a great thing. Notice the sun rises fresh every morning, however dark the night has been. It's as though God is refreshing the earth every day by His creative thinking.

If resurrection is anything, it is just that, to an infinite degree and we have one teaching us that always takes us forwards. "In Him we live and move and have our being". It says nothing about dying or being stationary or not 'being' any more, quite the opposite.

Missions have taken me forward because God gave the mandate, "Go into all the world". Now I don't know if I will ever travel more extensively on missions than I have so far but my 'world' has been very extensive because it engaged me with God and that in itself extended me in so many ways. True, I've preached in Uganda, Kenya, Rwanda, Ukraine and the USA after God took me to those places but it's not the amount of places I've been that matters but the experiences I've witnessed of God changing lives that counts.

A New Mission

It's my expanding world that matters to me, some quote John the Baptist saying, "I must decrease, He (Jesus) must increase." While I understand completely what they are trying to say, I also must say that I have grown along with everything that God gave me to do. Now my weak flesh decreased and the work of God in me increased but I must say that when I went on mission, I grew and enjoyed doing it. My faith has developed as a result of missions, so did my understanding of who I am in Christ Jesus. Like Job, I sometimes sit in awe and wonder at what God did, and say, "I KNOW, THAT YOU CAN DO ANYTHING!" Just watching God at work is a lesson in itself, it's amazing. I'm just speechless sometimes that God took me along with Him and I got to witness all those things.

So what's ahead?

Who knows? But if God is involved, **it's bound to be good.**

A New Mission

A New Mission

Mission means 'to send' and comes from the Latin text. It was first used about 'missionaries' in the 16th century who went abroad building schools and missions.

A New Mission

A New Mission

WWW.THEOVERCOMER.ORG.UK

Printed in Great Britain
by Amazon